Instant Lessons 2

Intermediate

Deirdre Howard-Williams
Mary Tomalin
Peter Watcyn-Jones
Edward Woods

Series Editor:
Peter Watcyn-Jones

PENGUIN ENGLISH

Pearson Education Limited
Edinburgh Gate
Harlow
Essex CM20 2JE, England
and Associated Companies throughout the world.

ISBN-13: 978-0-582-45146-9

First published 2000
Fifth impression 2007
Copyright © Deirdre Howard-Williams, Mary Tomalin, Peter Watcyn-Jones, Edward Woods 2000

The moral right of the authors has been asserted.

Every effort has been made to trace the copyright holders in every case. The publishers would be interested to hear from any not acknowledged.

Designed by Ferdinand Pageworks
Typeset by Pantek Arts
Illustrations by Sir Vin, Chris Pavely and Pantek Arts
Printed in China   SWTC/05

All rights reserved; no part of this publication may be reproduced, stored in a retrieval system, or transmitted in any form or by any means, electronic, mechanical, photocopying, recording or otherwise, without the prior written permission of the Publishers.

Photocopying notice
The pages in this book marked From *Instant Lessons 2 Intermediate* edited by Peter Watcyn-Jones © Penguin Books 2000 **Photocopiable** may be photocopied free of charge for classroom use by the purchasing individual or institution. This permission to copy does not extend to branches or additional schools of an institution. All other copying is subject to permission from the publisher.

Acknowledgements
The publishers make grateful acknowledgement to the following for permission to reproduce copyright material:

p 7, 'Portrait of Somerset Maugham' by Graham Sutherland, © Tate Gallery, London 2000; p 7, 'Portrait of the Journalist Sylvia von Harden' by Otto Dix, Photothèque des collections Mnam/Cci – Centre Georges Pompidou; p 7, 'Self Portrait' by Marie-Louise Elisabeth Vigée-Lebrun, courtesy of Ministero dei Beni e le Attività Culturali, Florence, © Fratelli Alinari, 2000; p 7, 'David Garrick' by Angelica Kauffmann (1741-1807), Burghley House Collection, Lincolnshire, UK/Bridgeman Art Library; p 23, 'Words, Wide Night' is taken from *The Other Country* by Carol Ann Duffy published by Anvil Press Poetry, 1990. New edition published, 1998; p 25, 'Coat' by Vicki Feaver is taken from *The Nation's Favourite Love Poems* published by BBC Books, 1997; p 47, 'Exclusive Recipe: Delia's Perfect Glass of Water' from *Private Eye Manual 1999*, Private Eye Magazine.

Published by Pearson Education Limited in association with Penguin Books Ltd, both companies being subsidiaries of Pearson plc.

For a complete list of the titles available from Penguin English please visit our website at www.penguinenglish.com, or write to your local Pearson Education office or to: Penguin English Marketing Department, Pearson Education, Edinburgh Gate, Harlow, Essex CM20 2JE.

Contents

Reading by Mary Tomalin

		page
1	Four portraits	6
2	Two-minute stories	10
3	Do you believe in ghosts?	14
4	Personality quiz	18
5	Two poems	22
6	Strange facts and quotations	26
7	Blood sports	30
8	Self-awareness	34
9	San Francisco	40
10	Recipes	46

Writing by Deirdre Howard-Williams

11	Are you green?	50
12	My CV	52
13	Writing home	54
14	A warm welcome	56
15	Where to go and what to see	58
16	In the news this week ...	60
17	Lots of letters	62
18	Telling stories	64
19	Create a word puzzle	66
20	Looking after yourself	68

Grammar by Edward Woods

		page
21	Past Simple v Present Perfect	70
22	Conditional 1	74
23	The article	78
24	Conditional 2	82
25	The passive	86
26	Comparisons	90
27	Modals 1: *must, have to*	94
28	Modals 2: *can, could, be able to*	98
29	Use of present tenses to express the future	102
30	Short answers with *so* or *neither/nor*	106

Vocabulary by Peter Watcyn-Jones

31	Character and personality adjectives	110
32	Words that sound the same (homophones)	112
33	How are you? How do you feel?	116
34	Phrasal verbs with *out*	118
35	Words and phrases with *make* and *do*	122
36	Pairs of words that are often confused	126
37	Prefixes	130
38	Giving definitions	134
39	Phrasal verbs with *up*	140
40	Types of people	142

Introduction

Instant Lessons 2 Intermediate is the second in a new series of photocopiable resource books for teachers and contains forty complete lessons for practising reading, writing, grammar and vocabulary. It is aimed at busy teachers who need an 'instant' or ready-made lesson. Although it is intended primarily for teachers new to the profession and non-native-speaking teachers, even the more experienced teacher should find a lot that is useful in the book.

Each activity contains material to be photocopied, usually one sheet or two, and clear step-by-step instructions to the teacher on preparation and organization. **Instant Lessons 2 Intermediate** can be used with adults and teenagers in a variety of different class situations to give extra practice in reading, writing, grammar and vocabulary in a fun and stimulating way.

Most of the lessons involve the students working in pairs or in small groups, which is an excellent way of making the learning process more dynamic and enjoyable.

Instant Lessons 2 Intermediate is not meant to replace a coursebook but is intended as a useful resource book to compliment any existing coursebook at this level. The teacher can simply pick and choose from it according to how useful and interesting a particular lesson is to his/her class.

How to use this book

Instant Lessons 2 Intermediate contains forty lessons. These are divided into four main sections:
Reading
Writing
Grammar
Vocabulary
with ten lessons per section.

Each lesson is complete in itself and consists of teacher's notes, a key (where appropriate) and one or more handout. Each lesson is intended to take 50–55 minutes and the very detailed teacher's notes give clear guidance on how many minutes each part of the lesson might take. There is also a comprehensive key, which again makes life a lot easier for the busy teacher. Finally, the teacher's notes are deliberately placed together with the handouts and, where possible, as a two-page spread – again to make the book 'user-friendly' and easy to teach from.

Choosing a lesson for your class

Lesson type
The teacher's notes for each lesson show at a glance the main teaching point of the lesson, making it a fairly easy task to find a suitable lesson to use quickly. The lessons are all at intermediate level and do not need to be done in sequence as each lesson is complete it itself. However, there is a slight progression in the level of difficulty, with the slightly easier lessons coming at the beginning of each section.

Preparing the activity before the lesson
The teacher's notes to each activity have a special section called Preparation. This section tells you exactly what you need to do before the class starts, i.e. how many pages to photocopy, how many copies are needed and if the copies need to be cut up in any way.

Organizing the activity in the classroom

Lesson plan
The teacher's notes for each lesson in **Instant Lessons 2 Intermediate** are divided into four main parts:
Introduction
Presentation
Practice
Conclusion
In addition, there is usually a section at the end with suggestions for homework.

Introduction
The teacher's notes start with suggestions as to how to introduce each activity. It is usually short – no more than 5 minutes.

Presentation
This is where the main teaching point is presented. It is nearly always teacher-led. It varies in length between 15 and 20 minutes.

Practice
This is always student-centred and is where the students get a chance to practise, where possible in a communicative way, what they have been taught in the previous section. Students normally work in pairs or groups. This is usually the longest part of the lesson (approximately 20–25 minutes).

Conclusion

Like the introduction, each lesson has a short activity at the end (5 minutes) to round it off. It is often used as a quick check to see if the students have assimilated the main points of the lesson.

Pair and group work

In most lessons students will spend much of their time working in pairs or groups. As such, a certain amount of classroom reorganization may be needed.

Where possible, rearrange the classroom slightly to make it easier for students to work in pairs or groups without disturbing others. Where this is not possible, students doing pairwork should work with the person sitting beside them or the person in front or behind (they just need to turn round). For group work, two students can easily turn their chairs round to face two others behind them. When you have an uneven number of students, most pair activities can be done by three people (if necessary, two students against one).

As far as possible, vary the pairs and groups so that students do not always work with the same people. It can sometimes be useful, for example, to mix stronger and weaker students in a small group so that they can help one another.

The enormous advantage of working in pairs and groups is that it gives everyone a chance to speak and in a non-threatening environment, i.e. with a fellow-student rather than in front of the teacher and the whole class. Students will learn from one another in a natural way that approximates more to the world outside and gets away from some of the constraints of the classroom. If this type of activity is new to them, it is useful to explain its advantages and to encourage them to take full advantage by participating as much as they can and sticking strictly to English!

The role of the teacher while this is going on is to facilitate communication by walking round the classroom, pausing briefly beside each pair/group. If all is going well, just encourage and move on. If things are not going so well, offer help and encouragement as needed to get students working well together.

While walking round, it is useful to have a small notebook or piece of paper on which you note down any common problems or persistent mistakes you hear. You can discuss these with the whole class during the feedback session – it is usually better to avoid saying who made each mistake as this can have a discouraging effect!

A note about photocopying

Since this is a photocopiable book with each activity containing one or more handout, it may be worth looking at ways of reducing the costs – both in terms of time and money. The material to be photocopied can be divided into two types: (a) handouts which the students write on, and (b) material which the students use but do not write on. Of the latter, many are cut up into cards.

For material that can be re-used, wherever possible try mounting it on cards and protecting it either by laminating it or (a cheaper solution) by keeping it in clear plastic folders. The extra initial effort will certainly pay off as subsequent photocopying costs and time will be reduced greatly.

Reading: Lessons 1–10

1 Four portraits

Aim	To compare written descriptions of people with their portraits.
Preparation	Copy the handouts on pages 7 and 9 – one copy per student.

Introduction *(5 minutes)*

Ask students to look at the four portraits on page 7 and try to guess the professions of the people portrayed. Check students understand *profession, portrait*. Elicit suggestions from students and write the suggestions on the board. You could briefly ask one or two students to give reasons for their choices. Example language: *He looks like a doctor. / He could be a doctor.*

Presentation *(10–15 minutes)*

Activity A Working in pairs, students read and discuss the questions. Give students time to read the questions, using their dictionaries if necessary, before checking they understand them. Check answers orally. Encourage discussion before giving answers. Example language: *The woman in picture b looks very hard. I don't think she's attractive.* Students will want to know the names of the people in the portraits and their painters:

a 'Portrait of Somerset Maugham' by Graham Sutherland (1949). Maugham was a famous English novelist.
b 'Portrait of the Journalist Sylvia von Harden' by Otto Dix (1926). Von Harden was German.
c 'Self-portrait' by Marie-Louise Elisabeth Vigee-Lebrun (1790). Vigee-Lebrun was a French portrait painter.
d 'David Garrick' by Angelica Kauffman (1764). Garrick was a famous English actor.

(continued on page 8)

Key

A 1 a writer b journalist c painter d actor
  2 pictures c and d
  3 a 1949 b 1926 c 1790 d 1764
  4 *Open answer*
  5 Probably c. There were very few women painters at that time.

(continued on page 8)

Teacher's notes

1 Four portraits

a   b

c   d

A Work in pairs and answer these questions.

1 Look at these four portraits. Guess the profession of each person. Choose from the following:

   painter   writer   journalist   actor

2 Two of these pictures were painted by women. Guess which ones.

3 Try to match these dates with the pictures.

   1764   1790   1949   1926

4 Which person do you think is the most attractive? Which person is the least attractive? Try to explain why.

5 Were you surprised by any of the answers to question 1? If so, why?

Teacher's notes

Practice (30 minutes)

Activity B In pairs, students read the descriptions of each portrait. There is something to disagree with in each description. They must say why they disagree. Students can use dictionaries if necessary. Then ask students: *Do you agree with the descriptions? Why not? What's wrong with them?* Example language: *He doesn't look as if he's had a happy life. / She looks intelligent but she doesn't look feminine. She looks masculine and hard.* Encourage students to use the structure: *looks as if* + verb. Write new language in sentences on the board.

Activity C In pairs, students answer the questions. You could ask students to write the answers. Students may need to use dictionaries. Check answers orally, correcting major errors. Encourage discussion for question 3. **Omit if lack of time.**

Activity D Students read and complete the notes on the French painter Marie-Louise Elisabeth Vigee-Lebrun (picture c) and actor David Garrick (picture d). Students should be able to guess from the context how to finish the sentences. Check answers orally, explaining where necessary. **Omit if lack of time.**

Conclusion (5 minutes)

Activity E Walk round and check what students have written.

Homework

Written answer to Activity B.

Key

B *Possible answers:*
Picture a: The man doesn't look as if he tries to help people. And he doesn't look as if he has had a happy life. He looks rather unhappy.
Picture b: This woman looks intelligent but she doesn't look feminine. She looks masculine and hard. She doesn't look like a wonderful mother. And she doesn't look as if she likes to make people happy.
Picture c: This woman's eyes aren't very wide because she is looking hard at something. She doesn't look frightened at all.
Picture d: This man certainly doesn't look stupid. He looks clever and interesting. He doesn't look as if he works with his hands. And he doesn't look too young to have children.

C *Possible answers:*
1 Because they get older, and sometimes because they worry a lot.
2 Because s/he is unhappy.
3 soft, gentle, sensitive, kind, loving
4 She is looking at herself because she is painting herself.
5 Work in a factory or on a farm, making something, for example a pot, work on the roads, house-painting
D 1 painted this picture/died in
2 becoming an actor/lived

1 Four portraits *(continued)*

B Work in pairs. Read these descriptions of the people in the pictures. Do you agree with the descriptions? If not, why not?

Picture a
This man's face has deep lines on it. He looks old and his mouth turns down at the corners. But he looks a wise old man, the kind of person who tries to help people. He looks as if he has had a happy life.

Picture b
This woman looks intelligent and at the same time very feminine. Perhaps she is the kind of woman who tries to hide her intelligence. She almost certainly is married with children and is probably a wonderful mother. She looks as if she likes to make people happy.

Picture c
The woman in this picture looks about twenty-three. She is very pretty and fresh-looking, with wide eyes. She is looking very hard at something, as if she is studying it carefully. But at the same time she looks frightened, as if she wants to run away.

Picture d
This man looks honest but stupid. He looks as if he doesn't have a thought in his head. He probably works with his hands, perhaps on a farm or something like that. He looks too young to have children. Perhaps as he gets older he will get wiser.

C Work in pairs. Answer these questions.

1. Why do people get lines on their face?
2. Why might someone's mouth turn down?
3. If someone is feminine, what kind of words would you use to describe them?
4. In portrait c, who is the woman looking at?
5. Give some examples of jobs where you work with your hands.

D Here are some short notes on the painter Marie-Louise Elisabeth Vigee-Lebrun (picture c) and the actor David Garrick (picture d). Read each text carefully and then complete the sentences. You will need more than one word to complete each sentence.

1. The French painter Marie-Louise Elisabeth Vigee-Lebrun was famous for her beauty, intelligence and charm. She was 35 when she .... She was kind to herself as she looks younger than 35 here. She was most famous for her pictures of women and children. She was born in 1755 and .... 1842.

2. David Garrick is seen as one of the greatest actors in the British theatre. He worked as a businessman before .... He was a theatre manager as well as an actor. He .... from 1717 to 1779.

E Write one or two sentences describing one of the people in the pictures.

Teacher's notes

2 Two-minute stories

Aim	To understand summaries of the plots of novels, plays and films.
Preparation	Copy the handouts on pages 11 and 13 – one copy per student.

Introduction *(5 minutes)*

Students write down the name of their favourite film and their favourite novel. Then they ask other students questions. For example: *Did anyone write down ... (name of film/book)? My favourite novel is ... What's yours?*

Presentation *(15 minutes)*

Activity A Students read the questions. Elicit/teach the words *century, summary*. Then students read the two summaries and in pairs answer the questions. Ask them not to use their dictionaries if possible. Elicit students' answers and the reasons for their answers. Elicit/teach the word *play*. They may know that the first story is Shakespeare's play, *Romeo and Juliet*. They probably won't know the second story, *Animal Farm*, a novel by George Orwell. Write new words on the board in sentences.

Practice *(25 minutes)*

Activity B In pairs, students read the summaries again. Then they do question 1. Encourage them to guess from context. Check answers orally, explaining where necessary. Then they do questions 2–6, using their dictionaries where necessary. Check answers orally. For questions 4, 5 and 6, encourage discussion. Correct major errors.

(continued on page 12)

Key

A Questions 1 and 2:
Summary 1 is the story of the play, *Romeo and Juliet*, by William Shakespeare (an Englishman). It was written in 1595 – at the end of the sixteenth century.
Summary 2 is the story of the novel, *Animal Farm*, by Englishman George Orwell. He wrote the book in 1945.

B 1 a rich
    b something that can make you ill or kill you if you eat or drink it
    c in the same way
    d someone powerful, who uses that power in a bad, cruel way

2 'R' has to leave the city because he has killed someone. If they find him, they will punish him, perhaps kill him. The young girl takes poison because she does not want to marry. She is already married to 'R'. The poison makes her appear dead for 48 hours. She knows her family will leave her and she can then leave the city with 'R'.
3 Because he believes that the girl is dead. In fact, she isn't; she took a poison which makes her appear dead.
4 Nothing has changed. Some animals have more power and money than others. They are not equal.
5 *Open answers*
6 *Open answer*

(continued on page 12)

2 Two-minute stories

A Read these summaries of two stories. Then, in pairs, answer the questions.

1 What century do you think the stories were written in? Why do you think this?

2 Do you know the names of these stories or who wrote them?

Two wealthy families living in the same city hate each other. 'R', a handsome young man from one of the families, falls in love with a young girl in
5 the other family. They marry secretly. Then 'R' accidentally kills a member of the other family and has to leave the city. Meanwhile, the young girl's family arrange a sudden marriage for her. To
10 prevent this, she takes a poison which makes her appear 'dead' for 48 hours. 'R' returns and sees her 'dead'. He kills himself. The young girl wakes up and, seeing her husband dead, she kills herself.

The animals on Mr Jones' farm
15 throw him and the other humans off the farm. With the pigs as leaders, they decide to manage the farm by themselves, and make sure that all the animals are treated equally. But as
20 time passes, the pigs become tyrants. They decide that 'all animals are equal but some are more equal than others.' A good and kind horse is killed. Finally, the pigs agree with Mr Jones
25 that he can help manage the farm.

B Work in pairs. Read the summaries again and answer the questions.

1 Guess the meaning of these words:

   a wealthy (line 1) **b** poison (line 10) **c** equally (line 20) **d** tyrant (line 21)

2 Why does 'R' have to leave the city? Why does the young girl take poison?

3 Why does 'R' kill himself?

4 Explain this sentence: 'All animals are equal but some are more equal than others.'

5 Which story do you find more interesting? Why? Which is sadder?

6 Which do you think is more realistic?

From *Instant Lessons 2 Intermediate* edited by Peter Watcyn-Jones © Penguin Books 2000

Teacher's notes

Activity C Elicit/pre-teach these words: *shipwrecked, desert island, hit, iceberg*. Students read the question and the summaries. In pairs, they discuss the question. Then elicit students' answers and the reasons for their answers. Correct major errors.
Summary 1 tells the story of *Lord of the Flies* by William Golding (1954). Summary 2 tells the true story of the *Titanic*, a ship which sank in 1914. A famous film was made of the story in 1998. Students may have seen it.

Activity D In pairs, students read the summaries again and answer questions 1–5. Check answers orally, explaining where necessary. Questions 4 and 5: Encourage discussion. For question 5, check students understand the words *optimistic/pessimistic*. Write new words on the board in sentences.
Optional Extension In small groups students choose a novel/film and write a summary of it. As in these stories, they use the Present Simple.

Conclusion *(5 minutes)*

Activity E In pairs, students choose new titles for stories A2 and C1.

Homework

Written answers to Activity D, questions 4 and 5.

Key

C Summary 2 is true. It tells the story of the *Titanic*, a ship which sank in 1914.
D 1 Story 2. The film was called *Titanic*.
   2 Because they have become savage and cruel. They have killed two boys.
   3 a in the north Atlantic and south Pacific
      b in the sea, in hot/tropical parts of the world
      c on ships, trains, planes, buses and in cars
      d on farms
      e in chemists and plants
   4 *Open answers*
   5 *Open answers*
E *Possible answers:*
   Pig Farm/Some Animals are More Equal Than Others
   Shipwreck/Savage Island

2 Two-minute stories (continued)

C Work in pairs. Read these summaries of two stories. One of them is true. Which one is it? Why do you think this?

> A group of boys are shipwrecked on a desert island. They become savage and cruel and kill two boys in the group. Finally they are rescued, but the boys will never be the same again.

> A huge ship starts its journey across the Atlantic Ocean. It is the biggest ship ever built. People believe that nothing can sink it. But during the night it hits an iceberg and sinks. Of the 2200 passengers, only 700 survive.

D Work in pairs. Read the stories in Activity C again. Answer the questions.

1 Which story in Activity C became a very famous film in 1998?
2 Why will the boys in story 1 'never be the same again'?
3 Where do you find these?
   a icebergs   b desert islands   c passengers   d pigs   e poison
4 Which of the four stories try to tell us something important about human beings? What do they try to tell us?
5 Are these four stories optimistic or pessimistic? What kind of stories do you prefer?

E Choose new titles for stories A2 and C1.

From *Instant Lessons 2 Intermediate* edited by Peter Watcyn-Jones © Penguin Books 2000

Teacher's notes

3 Do you believe in ghosts?

Aim	To understand a real-life ghost story presented as a jigsaw reading.
Preparation	Copy the handouts on pages 15 and 17 – one copy per student. If required, cut the story in Activity A into four sections.

Introduction (5 minutes)

Write these words on the board: *college, door, shaking, ghost, knocking, haunted, terror, to expect, to chat, to interrupt, central heating, occasion, absolute, priest*. Tell students they are going to read a story containing these words. Check students understand the words. Ask: *What do you think the story is about?* Elicit suggestions from them.

Presentation (10–15 minutes)

Activity A Students have to put sections a, b, c and d into the right order to tell a story. You can do the activity in this way:
Students work in groups of four. Cut the story in Activity A into four sections, a, b, c and d. Give each member of a group one of the four sections. Each student reads his/her section but must not show it to the other students. Then, as a group, students have to put the story together. They do this by telling each other about their section. They can read it to the rest of the group if they wish. Students use their dictionaries where necessary but shouldn't try to understand every word.

Alternatively, students can do the activity in pairs. In this case, give one student sections a and d. Give the other student sections b and c. If you don't wish to cut the story up, students can simply look at Activity A and do it from the page, but the group activity is more useful, as students have to communicate with each other. Check answers orally, explaining where necessary.

(continued on page 16)

Key

A d, b, a, c

(continued on page 16)

3 Do you believe in ghosts?

A Put these paragraphs into the right order so that they tell a story.

A Cambridge Haunting

a

Some months later, Andrew Murison, a financial manager at the college, was in the same room. He says, 'It was about 11.45. Suddenly I heard a knocking from beneath the window. There is no central heating there. I had already noticed how cold it was. I thought this was very strange because the fire was still burning.'

On another occasion, another waiter, Paul Cooke, noticed a wooden door in the room shaking violently. When at last he succeeded in opening it, there was no one on the other side. He interrupted a dinner to tell the college priest.

b

Both men described the ghost as human-sized, but said it was impossible to see its face clearly or say whether it was a man or woman. It travelled about 30 centimetres off the ground. In the dark room the ghost seemed very bright and both waiters felt suddenly cold. Mr Davies said, 'I was not frightened but, at the same time, I did not want to get too close.'

c

Graham Ward says, 'I saw the absolute terror on his face, so I don't doubt something happened. All the people who have seen and heard these things are completely reliable men.' He feels sure that there is a ghost in the college. What do you think?

This story is taken from an article that appeared in *The Times* newspaper on December 19th, 1997.

d

Cambridge University is one of the oldest universities in England. So, if you believe in ghosts, perhaps you would expect to see a ghost there. In 1997 there were several reports of a ghost at one of the Cambridge colleges. The college priest, Graham Ward, is certain that the college is haunted. This is the story.

In April 1997, two waiters, Matthew Speller and Paul Davies, went into a room near the kitchen to get some plates. Mr Speller says, 'We were chatting when we both saw something move slowly across the room. I just looked at Paul and said, "Did you see that?"'

Teacher's notes

Practice *(30 minutes)*

Activity B In pairs, students read the text in the correct order. Students answer the questions, using dictionaries where necessary. Then check answers orally, explaining where necessary. Write new words on the board in sentences.
Optional Extension In pairs, students play the two waiters and say what they saw. They will need to read part of the story more carefully to do this.

Activity C Students work in pairs. Question 1: They read the story and guess the meaning of the words from the context. Check answers orally, explaining where necessary. Question 2: They read the story again and correct the sentences, using dictionaries. Check answers orally, explaining where necessary.

Activity D In pairs, students complete the sentences and say which story they are from. **Omit if lack of time.**

Activity E (Optional Extension) By now, students will have acquired enough vocabulary to have this discussion. Useful language: *Perhaps they saw ... / They probably saw ... / It could have been (his imagination).*

Conclusion *(5 minutes)*

Activity F Walk round and check what students have written.

Homework

A written answer to Activity E.

Key

B 1 Two people, waiters Matthew Speller and Paul Davies.
   2 It was human-sized, but they couldn't see if it was a man or a woman and they couldn't see its face clearly. It travelled about 30 centimetres off the ground and was very bright.
   3 Two people, Andrew Murison and Paul Cooke.
   4 Because he says the people who saw and heard these things are very reliable men. And there was terror on Paul Cooke's face when he told him the story.
   5 Yes, it is true. The story was taken from an article in *The Times* newspaper.

C 1 security officer: a man employed to make sure that a place is safe
archway: an arch is a curved structure at the top of a door, window etc.; an archway is the place where you can walk under an arch
figure: a human shape
investigate: to try and find out about something, especially a crime or accident
   2 a The officer saw a man walk through <u>a wall</u>. (There used to be an archway in that part of the wall.)
      b The man went through the wall and <u>disappeared</u>.
      c At night the security officers often <u>hear footsteps</u>.

D 1 shaking/Story 1
   2 through/Story 2
   3 haunted/Story 1
   4 terror/Story 1
   5 footsteps/Story 2
   6 knocking/Story 1

3 Do you believe in ghosts? (continued)

B Work in pairs. Read the story in the correct order. Answer these questions.

1. How many people actually saw the ghost?
2. Describe the ghost.
3. How many people heard something strange?
4. Why does the college priest believe that there is a ghost?
5. Is this story true? How do you know?

C Work in pairs. Here is another true ghost story. Read it and answer the questions.

WESTDOWN POLICE COUNTY CONSTABULARY

STATEMENT

In 1972, in a big mansion called Bramshill House in Hampshire, England, a <u>security officer</u> saw a man walking on the path outside. The officer, Mr William Chalk, said, 'The man came in through the open door and went straight through the wall opposite. The back of my neck went cold and I hurried round the corner to see where he had gone but he had disappeared. Later I found out that there used to be an <u>archway</u> there.' According to the local police newspaper, in 1980 a <u>figure</u> appeared and then vanished in a room. At night, the security officers hear footsteps so often that they no longer go to <u>investigate</u>.

---

1. Guess the meaning of the underlined words (lines 1, 4, 5 and 6).
2. Correct the mistakes in these sentences.
   a The officer saw a man walk through an archway.
   b The man went through the wall and then appeared again.
   c At night the security officers often see someone vanish and then appear again.

D Complete the following sentences without looking at the texts. Are the sentences from story 1 or story 2? Tick (✔) the right column.

	Story 1	Story 2
1 He saw a door ....ing violently.		
2 The man went straight .... the wall opposite.		
3 Graham Ward is certain that the college is		
4 I saw the .... on his face.		
5 At night the security officers often hear		
6 I heard a ....ing from beneath the window.		

E Do you believe that the people in these two stories saw ghosts? Give reasons for your opinion.

F Complete one of these sentences.
I believe in ghosts because ...
I don't believe in ghosts because ...

From *Instant Lessons 2 Intermediate* edited by Peter Watcyn-Jones © Penguin Books 2000

Teacher's notes

4 Personality quiz

Aim	To answer a multiple choice questionnaire about personality.
Preparation	Copy the handouts on pages 19 and 21 – one copy per student.

Introduction *(5 minutes)*

Elicit/teach the words *to achieve, achievement*. Ask students: *Which is more important to you, love or achievement?* Elicit some answers. Elicit/teach the words *personality, quiz*. Tell students you are going to give them a personality quiz to find out which is more important. Ask them to write down their predictions for the three students nearest them. For example: *I think achievement is more important for Carlos than love.*

Presentation *(20 minutes)*

Activity A Students read the quiz (but not the Quiz Scores section) and try to guess what the underlined words mean. Ask them not to use their dictionaries if possible. Then check orally, helping students to see how they can use the context to help them guess. Students then read the Introduction to the quiz again. Make sure they understand they can only choose a or b for each question. Then students do the quiz, using their dictionaries where necessary. When they have completed the quiz, point out the section on Quiz Scores. Elicit/teach the words *score, mark, independence, oriented (achievement-oriented/love-oriented = to be concerned with achievement/love)*. Then students read the Quiz Scores section and mark themselves.

(continued on page 20)

Key

A 1 honest: someone who is honest does not lie or steal
team: a group of people who work together to do a particular job
aim: a purpose that you hope to achieve
potential: possible
responsible: someone who is responsible does his/her duty

(continued on page 20)

4 Personality quiz

A 1 Read this quiz and try to guess the meaning of the underlined words
   2 Now do the quiz and find out which is more important to you: love or achievement. Do not look at the Quiz Scores yet.

Personality Quiz

**For each question choose only one answer, a or b.
Try and be <u>honest</u> with yourself.**

1 You have a choice of two jobs. Which job will you choose?
   a Working as part of a <u>team</u> for less money.
   b Working alone for more money.
2 When you play a competitive game, which of these do you do?
   a Try very hard to win.
   b Just enjoy playing – winning doesn't matter to you.
3 Which is more important to you?
   a To have people's respect.
   b To have people's love.
4 Which is more important to you?
   a To make sure that those around you are happy.
   b To give yourself <u>aims</u> in life and to achieve them.
5 You have started a new job. Which do you do first?
   a Look around for <u>potential</u> friends.
   b Make sure you know who the important people are.
6 Which is more important to you?
   a To be strong and <u>responsible</u>.
   b To be warm and friendly.
7 Which of these statements is more true for you?
   a I like to have people's good opinion.
   b I don't care very much what people think of me.

✷ ✷ ✷ ✷ ✷ ✷ ✷ ✷ ✷ ✷ ✷ ✷ ✷ ✷ ✷ ✷ ✷

Quiz Scores
Give yourself these marks for your answers:

1a: 1	2a: 2	3a: 2	4a: 1	5a: 1	6a: 2	7a: 1
1b: 2	2b: 1	3b: 1	4b: 2	5b: 2	6b: 1	7b: 2

Now add up your marks for the total score.
- 12–14: You need to achieve and change things. You are a 'doer', and have a need for independence and the respect of others.
- 10–11: Your need for love and your need to achieve are about equal.
- 7–9: You are a love-oriented person. Family and friends are more important to you than achievements. You like to give and receive warmth and love.

From *Instant Lessons 2 Intermediate* edited by Peter Watcyn-Jones © Penguin Books 2000

Teacher's notes

Practice *(25 minutes)*

Activity B Working in pairs, students answer and discuss the questions, using their dictionaries where necessary. Question 4: Students ask the three people whose results they predicted: *What result did you get?* They might want to discuss this with them! Then check answers orally, explaining where necessary. Correct major errors. Write new words on the board in sentences.

Activity C Students read the text and answer the questions, using their dictionaries. (*Reference:* the letter you ask a former employer to write, recommending you for a new job.) Check question 1 orally, explaining where necessary. Ask if they think Neil is love-oriented or achievement-oriented. Encourage a brief discussion about question 2 as a whole class activity, then put the class into groups of four to make a decision on question 2 and continue onto question 3.

Activity D Working in pairs, students write answers to these questions, using dictionaries where necessary. Check answers orally, explaining where necessary. **Omit if lack of time.**

Conclusion *(5 minutes)*

Activity E Students answer the questions. Have a class discussion about their answers. Do most of the class share the same opinion?

Homework

Students write a paragraph or two expanding on their answers in Activity E.

Key

B 1 *Open answer*
   2 *Open answer*
   3 love: companionship, warmth, friendship, to care for, to have/feel affection (for)
      achievement: independence, power, action, goal, aim, success

C 1 Because his work was unsatisfactory for two years. This is because two members of his family are chronically ill.
   2 *Open answer*
   3 *Open answer*

D 1 a below standard
     b the situation will not improve
   2 They design machines, cars, trains, electrical equipment, roads, bridges, etc.

4 Personality quiz (continued)

B Work in pairs. Answer these questions.

1 Do you agree with the quiz result? If not, why not?

2 Would you like to be different (for example, love-oriented rather than achievement-oriented) or are you happy as you are?

3 Put these words into two groups: *love* or *achievement*

companionship   warmth   independence   power   action
friendship   goal   to care for   aim   success   to have/feel affection (for)

4 Did other people in the class get the result you predicted? Ask them!

C Read the text then answer the questions.

> You are the head of the engineering department in a large company. You have asked Neil Kennet, an employee in the department, to leave because his work has been below standard for the past two years. You know this is because two members of his family are ill. You also know that they are chronically ill – the situation will not improve. Before asking Neil to leave, you had a number of discussions with him in order to try and help him, but they were not successful. Neil has just left the company and applied for another job. He has written to you asking for a reference.

1 Why was Neil asked to leave?

2 Imagine you are the head of the department. Discuss what you would write in Neil's reference.

3 Do you think reference letters are a useful way for a company to find out if you will be a good employee?

D Work in pairs. Answer these questions.

1 Read through the text in Activity C again and find the following:
a a two-word phrase for 'unsatisfactory'
b an explanation for 'chronically'.

2 What kind of work do engineers do?

E Do you think most men are love-oriented or achievement-oriented? What about women?

Teacher's notes

5 Two poems

Aim	To understand and compare two poems.
Preparation	Copy the handouts on pages 23 and 25 – one copy per student.

Introduction *(5 minutes)*

Put the following words on the board: *night, hills, room, distance, wide, pleasurable, sad*. Check that students understand the words. Tell them that the words come from a poem that they are going to read. Elicit ideas of what the poem might be about.

Presentation *(20 minutes)*

Activity A In pairs, students read the poem and complete the gaps. Allow them to use their dictionaries. You might want to pre-teach *tense* (= *form of a verb that shows past/present/future*). Then check answers orally, explaining where necessary why a word would not fit in the gap. But if students offer a word that would fit (even if it is not the word in the poem), congratulate them! Then go through the poem and check students understand it. Write new words on the board in sentences.

Activity B Students answer the questions in pairs. Allow them to use their dictionaries to help them with the questions, but at some point check they understand them. Then go through answers orally, explaining where necessary. Question 6: Read the poem to the students. Finally, in pairs, they can take turns to read sections of the poem.

(continued on page 24)

Key

A moon, desire, reach, words
B 1 b
   2 ... this wide night and the distance between us / ... that you cannot hear / ... the dark hills I must cross to reach you
   3 a the fact that I am thinking of you
      b to be in love or the poem
   4 the Present Continuous
   5 *Open answer*
   6 *Open answer*

(continued on page 24)

5 Two poems

A Work in pairs. Read the poem and think of a word to put in the gaps.

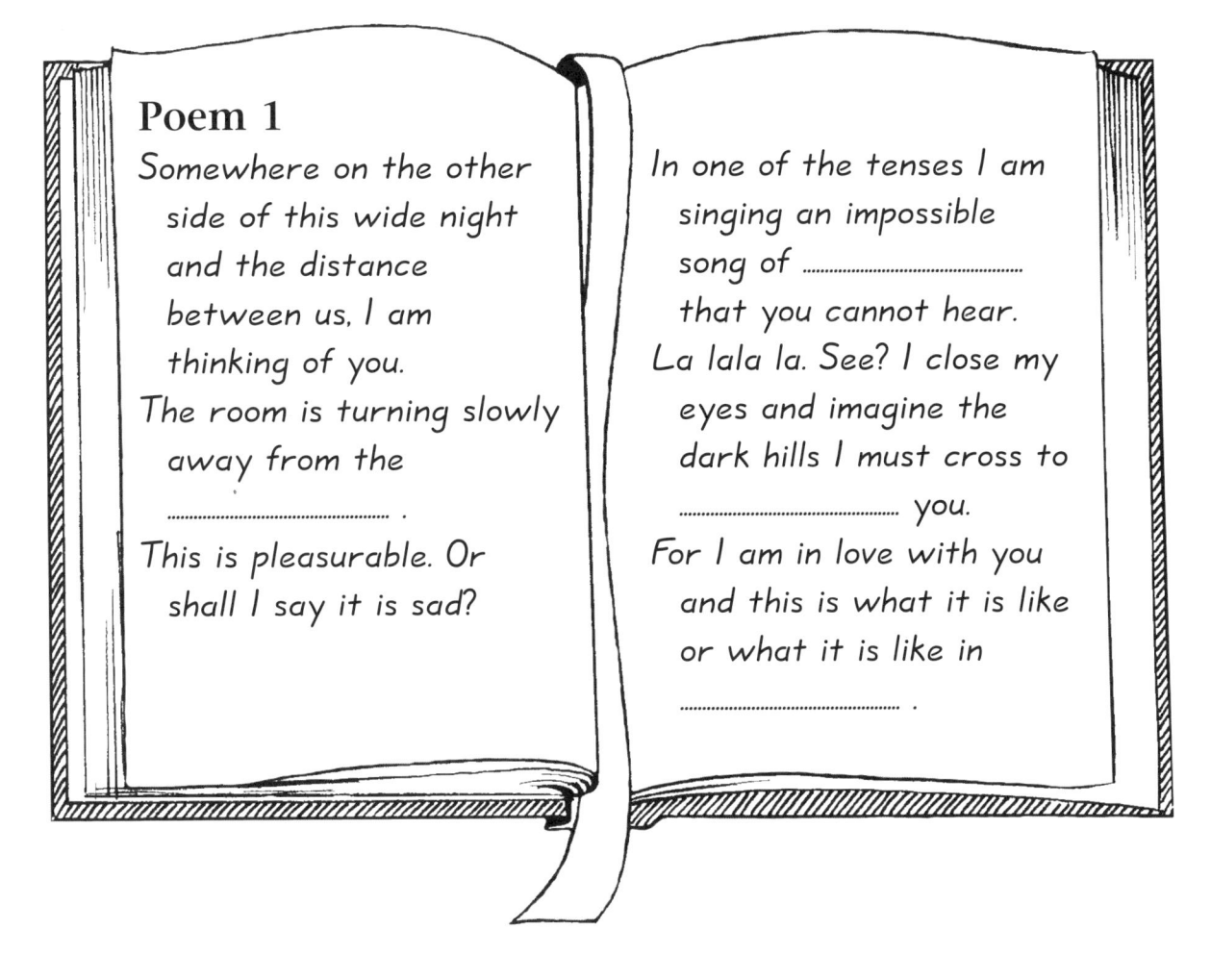

Poem 1

Somewhere on the other
 side of this wide night
and the distance
 between us, I am
 thinking of you.
The room is turning slowly
 away from the
 ....
This is pleasurable. Or
 shall I say it is sad?
In one of the tenses I am
 singing an impossible
 song of ....
 that you cannot hear.
La lala la. See? I close my
 eyes and imagine the
 dark hills I must cross to
 .... you.
For I am in love with you
 and this is what it is like
 or what it is like in
 ....

B Work in pairs. Read poem 1 again and answer these questions.

1 What is the poem about?
 a unhappiness
 b desire
 c the night

2 What words does the poet use to show there is a separation?

3 What does *this* mean in these sentences?
 a *This* is pleasurable.
 b For I am in love with you and *this* is what it is like ...

4 What tense is the third line of the poem in?

5 How does the poem make you feel?
 a Sad and lonely.
 b Happy in a strange way.
 c It doesn't do anything to me.

6 Read the poem aloud. Does it feel any different when you read it in this way?

Teacher's notes

Practice *(20 minutes)*

Activity C As in Activity A, students read the poem in pairs and complete the gaps, using their dictionaries. Check answers orally, congratulating students if they have thought of a suitable word. Again, go through the poem checking comprehension.

Activity D In pairs, students answer the questions. If you wish, pre-teach *relationship, regret, title*. Encourage discussion and correct major errors. Question 4: When students have given their titles, tell them the real titles (Poem 1: *Words/Wide Night*. Poem 2: *Coat*). Ask students: *What do you think of the titles?* Question 5: Again, read the poem aloud to the students first.

Conclusion *(5 minutes)*

Ask students to try and learn the first verse of one of the poems.

Homework

Written answers to Activity D.

Key

C coat, move, clothes, warm

D 1 *Possible answer:* Perhaps the poet felt that the person wanted or needed too much. Perhaps the person was rather jealous.
 2 I am lonely; I need some love.
 3 Poem 2. The poet misses the person in the poem. S/he regrets that they have split up, and wants him/her back.
 4 *Open answer, but real titles are:*
   Poem 1: Words/Wide Night
   Poem 2: Coat
 5 *Open answer*
 6 Both poems were written by women. Poem 1 was written by Carol Anne Duffy (1955–). Poem 2 was written by Vicki Feaver (1943–).

5 Two poems (continued)

C Work in pairs. Read this poem and think of a word to put in the gaps.

Poem 2

1
Sometimes I have wanted to throw you off like a heavy ....

2
Sometimes I have said you would not let me breathe or ....

3
But now that I am free to choose light .... or none at all

4
I feel the cold and all the time I think how .... it used to be.

D Work in pairs. Answer these questions.
1. What do you think the relationship between the poet and the person in poem 2 was like?
2. What does the poet mean by these words: 'I feel the cold ...'.
3. Of the two poems, which is about regret? What does the poet regret?
4. Choose a title for each of the poems.
5. Read poem 2 aloud. Which poem do you like best? Why?
6. Who do you think wrote each of the poems, a man or a woman? Why?

Teacher's notes

6 Strange facts and quotations

Aim	To categorize and guess the source of quotations and facts.
Preparation	Copy the handouts on pages 27 and 29 – one copy per student.

Introduction (5 minutes)

Teach the word *cricket (= insect)*. Write these two sentences on the board:
Crickets hear things through their knees.
I'm not afraid to die. I just don't want to be there when it happens.
Elicit/teach the words *fact, quotation*. (A quotation is something that someone else has said or written.) Ask students: *Which sentence is a fact? Which sentence is a quotation?* Elicit students' answers, then tell them the answer. (Answer: The first sentence is a fact, the second is a quotation by the American film director Woody Allen.)

Presentation (15 minutes)

Activity A Students work in pairs. Ask them not to use their dictionaries if possible. Explain that they can probably group the sentences by noting certain words. Explain that these are all quotations but the names of the people who said them are not given because students probably haven't heard of the speakers. Check students' answers orally, explaining where necessary. Write new words on the board in sentences.

Activity B Again, students do the activity in pairs. This time, encourage them to use their dictionaries. Check students understand the questions. Question 1: Ask students: *When did King George V [the Fifth] live?* (The answer is next to his name: *1865–1936*.) The correct answer to this question is quotation 5, but praise students who can justify other quotations. Question 2: Encourage students to discuss. Check answers orally, explaining where necessary. Correct major errors. **Omit 3 and 4 if lack of time.**

Practice (25 minutes)

Activity C Working in pairs, students read the question, using their dictionaries. Elicit/pre-teach these words (they're all the names of animals): *butterfly, owl, elephant, pig, lobster, baboon*. Then ask students for their answer and why they think this. Finally, give them the correct answer, which is number 10: *Men outnumber women in prisons in Britain by thirty to one*.

(continued on page 28)

Key

A 1 Food: 2, 6   Money: 1, 7   Children: 3, 5
     Marriage: 4, 8
B 1 Quotation 5
  2 *Possible answer:* I like quotation 6 because it's clever. It's a play on words. And I like quotation 8 because I think it's true. Men don't like talking about their feelings.
  3 This quotation is a 'play on words'. In other words, the word *light* has two meanings in this sentence. In the first sentence, *a light eater* means the person *doesn't eat much*. In the second sentence, *light* means *daylight*.
  4 Quotation 7: Rich people pay other people to help them avoid taxes. 'Little people' (ordinary people) have to pay.
     Quotation 8: Women often say that men don't like talking about their feelings. So if a woman says to her husband late at night, 'Let's talk about our relationship,' the man will quickly go to sleep!
C Fact 10: Men outnumber women in prisons in Britain by thirty to one.

(continued on page 28)

6 Strange facts and quotations

A Below are eight quotations by famous people. Put them into groups under the following headings.

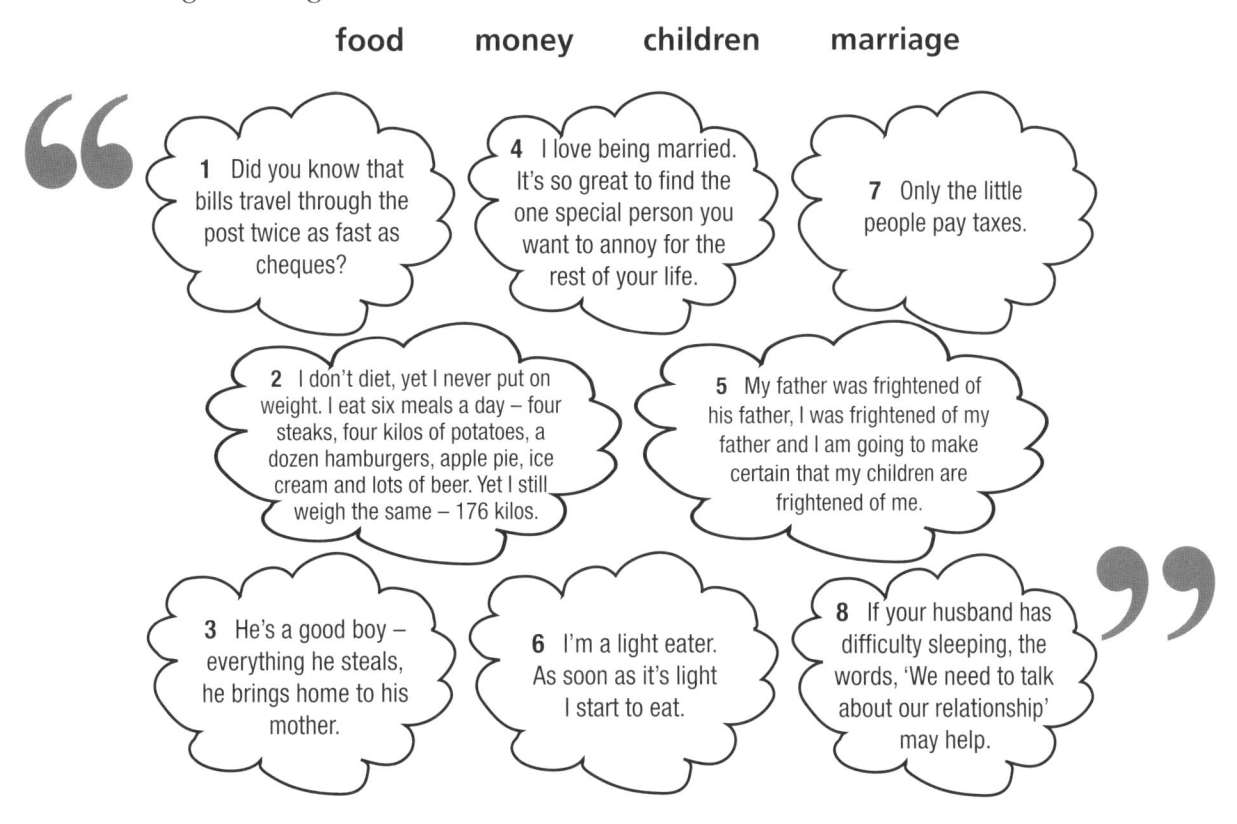

food   money   children   marriage

1 Did you know that bills travel through the post twice as fast as cheques?

2 I don't diet, yet I never put on weight. I eat six meals a day – four steaks, four kilos of potatoes, a dozen hamburgers, apple pie, ice cream and lots of beer. Yet I still weigh the same – 176 kilos.

3 He's a good boy – everything he steals, he brings home to his mother.

4 I love being married. It's so great to find the one special person you want to annoy for the rest of your life.

5 My father was frightened of his father, I was frightened of my father and I am going to make certain that my children are frightened of me.

6 I'm a light eater. As soon as it's light I start to eat.

7 Only the little people pay taxes.

8 If your husband has difficulty sleeping, the words, 'We need to talk about our relationship' may help.

B Work in pairs. Answer these questions about the quotations.

1 Guess which of the quotations was said by King George V of England (1865–1936). Why do you think this?
2 Which quotation do you like the best? Why?
3 There are two meanings to the word *light* in quotation 6. What are they?
4 Explain the meaning of quotations 7 and 8.

C Work in pairs. All these statements are true, except one. Guess which one is false.

1 In California it is illegal to kill a butterfly.
2 An owl can turn its head in a complete circle.
3 Elephants are unable to jump into the air.
4 In nearly every language in the world, the word for mother begins with an 'm' sound.
5 A pig was executed in a public hanging in 1386 for the murder of a child.
6 Empress Elizabeth of Russia had fifteen thousand dresses.
7 Lobsters have blue blood.
8 In ancient Egypt they taught baboons to serve at their tables.
9 Bamboo can grow over three feet (90cm) in twenty-four hours.
10 Men outnumber women in prisons in Britain by twenty to one.

From *Instant Lessons 2 Intermediate* edited by Peter Watcyn-Jones © Penguin Books 2000

Teacher's notes

Activity D Give students time to read the questions, using their dictionaries. Then check they understand the questions. Encourage students not to look at the quotations for the first part of questions 1, 2 and 4. For question 5, encourage students to discuss. Check answers orally, correcting major errors. Write new words on the board in sentences.

Activities E and F Working in pairs, students answer the questions, using their dictionaries. Then check answers orally, explaining where necessary. **Omit if lack of time.**

Conclusion *(5 minutes)*

Activity G Walk round and check what students have written.

Homework

Any omitted activities.

Key

D 1/2 Six: butterfly, owl, elephants, pig, lobsters, baboons
   3 (People eat different animals in different countries.) Butterflies and owls can fly.
   4 Four: California, Russia, Egypt, Britain
   5 *Open answer*
E Quotations: 2, 3   Strange facts: 1, 4
F 1a Muhammad Ali is a famous American heavyweight boxing champion. He first became famous in the 1960s under the name Cassius Clay. He became the World Heavyweight Champion in 1964 and changed his name to Muhammad Ali that same year. He won the World Heavyweight Champion title twice more, in 1974 and 1978. He is the only heavyweight boxer ever to have won the title three times.

1b Elizabeth I [the First] was Queen of England from 1533 to 1603. She was very clever and made England a very strong country.
2 Muhammad Ali: quotation 3 (Muhammad Ali was talking about his style of boxing.)
Elizabeth I: quotation 2

6 Strange facts and quotations *(continued)*

D Work in pairs. Answer these questions.

1 How many of the statements in Activity C are about animals? Try not to look.

2 Now check. Were you right? Now don't look again. Can you remember any of them? Try and repeat a fact without looking!

3 Which animals would people in your country eat? Which animals can fly?

4 How many places are mentioned? Again, try not to look. Then check.

5 Which three facts do you think are the strangest? Explain why.

E Work in pairs. Which of these are quotations? Which are strange facts?

1 The ancient Chinese used to organize fights between crickets.

2 I have the heart and mind of a man in the body of a feeble woman.

3 Dance like a butterfly, sting like a bee.

4 The French writer Victor Hugo wrote a novel containing a sentence 823 words long.

F Work in pairs. Answer these questions.

1 Who were these people?
  a Muhammad Ali (1942–)
  b Queen Elizabeth I (1533–1603)

2 Guess which quotations from Activity E are theirs. Explain why you think this.

G Work in pairs. Don't look at the activities. Try and write down one strange fact and one quotation. Then look at the activities and check.

From *Instant Lessons 2 Intermediate* edited by Peter Watcyn-Jones © Penguin Books 2000

Teacher's notes

7 Blood sports

Aim	To read a text debating the pros and cons of a political and moral issue.
Preparation	Copy the handouts on pages 31 and 33 – one copy per student. If required, cut up the text in Activity A into five sections.

Introduction (5 minutes)

Write the phrase *blood sports* on the board and ask students: *What are blood sports?* (= *the killing of animals for pleasure*). Elicit answers from students and explain if necessary. Ask students for examples of *blood sports*. Write the word *fox-hunting* on the board and ask students: *What is fox-hunting?* If necessary, teach the words *fox, to hunt*. Ask: *In what country do people go fox-hunting?* (Answer: *Britain. Dogs and horse riders chase a fox and kill it.*) Also teach the word *upper classes* (= *people who belong to the highest social class/group*).

Presentation (15 minutes)

Activity A In this activity, students have to put sections a, b, c, d and e into the right order. You can do the activity in this way:
Students work in groups of five. Cut the text in Activity A into five sections: a, b, c, d and e. Give each member of a group one of the five sections. Each student reads his/her section, using a dictionary where necessary. S/he must not show it to the other students. Then, as a group, students have to put the story together. They do this by telling each other about their section. They can read it to the rest of the group if they wish. Tell students they should not try and understand every word. Pre-teach these words: *argument (for/against/anti), to abolish, cruel, supporter*.
Alternatively, students can do the activity in pairs. In this case, give one student sections a, b and c. Give the other student sections d and e. If you don't wish to cut the text up, students simply read the paragraphs on the page and number them in the correct order. The group activity is probably the most useful, however, as students have to communicate with each other. Check answers orally, asking students to explain how they got to the answer. The correct order is: b, e, c, a, d. There are certain sentences in the text that signal the next paragraph. For example, paragraph e: *What are the arguments for and against?* and paragraph a: *Supporters of blood sports have several answers to this*.

(*continued on page 32*)

Key	
A b, e, c, a, d	(*continued on page 32*)

7 Blood sports

A Read the paragraphs and put them into the correct order.

a

Supporters of blood sports have several answers to this. They say that the suffering of the animal lasts a very short time. In the case of fox-hunting, they say that foxes destroy the countryside and must be killed anyway. Other ways of killing them are just as cruel. They argue that blood sports are a way of life for many people. For country people in Britain, fox-hunting can be an important social occasion. Finally, they argue that sports such as bullfighting and fox-hunting employ thousands of people. For this reason alone they must continue.

b

Man is a hunter. True or false? Certainly, for thousands of years man hunted from necessity, and in some parts of the world he still does. In other parts, the practice continues, not from necessity, but because hunting gives pleasure to the hunter. In Britain the upper classes are famous for their love of fox-hunting. In this sport, a fox is chased by dogs and the dogs are chased by horses and riders, eager to see the fox killed.

c

Blood sports are cruel, say those who are against blood sports. They ask how we can allow such cruelty in the twenty-first century. In fox-hunting, for example, the hunters create terror in the fox before killing it. In bullfighting, the bull is killed slowly and painfully. To kill in order to eat is acceptable. But it is not acceptable to kill for pleasure. That is cruelty, goes the argument.

d

The issue of fox-hunting in Britain has brought people out on the streets. Country people have marched in London. Anti-blood-sport campaigners have marched against the country people. Who will succeed in the end? At present it is impossible to say.

e

Fox-hunting is known as a 'blood sport' – in other words, the killing of animals for pleasure. Other blood sports include bullfighting (Spain and Latin American countries) and cockfighting (many countries but particularly Asia). Today, many people want to abolish such practices. Blood sport supporters, however, are determined to fight back. What are the arguments for and against?

Teacher's notes

Practice *(30 minutes)*

Activity B In pairs, students read the paragraphs in the correct order and answer the questions. Check students understand the questions. Elicit/teach *in favour of (= 'for ' something)*. Check answers orally. Check written answers for question 2. Correct major errors.

Activities C, D and E Students do these activities in pairs, using dictionaries if necessary. Check answers orally, explaining where necessary. Write new words on the board in sentences. **Omit if lack of time.**

Activity F Students discuss these questions in small groups or pairs. Alternatively, the questions could be discussed as a whole class activity. Correct major errors.

Conclusion *(5 minutes)*

Activity G Check answers orally. If students suggest some surprising words, ask them to justify their answers.

Homework

Students can write an answer to Activity F, question 3. They can also do any omitted exercises.

Key

B 1 against: paragraph c
      for: paragraph a
   2 **Arguments against blood sports**
      Blood sports are cruel.
      It is not acceptable to kill for pleasure.
      Arguments in favour of blood sports
      The suffering of the animal lasts a very short time.
      Foxes must be killed anyway. Other ways of killing them are just as cruel.
      Blood sports are a way of life.
      Blood sports employ thousands of people.
   3 The author is simply giving the arguments, without giving a personal opinion.

C 1a, 2b, 3a, 4a
D a3, b1, c2
E 1 ... man hunted because he had to in order to eat.
   2 ... people have marched in the streets to show that they are either for or against fox-hunting.
   3 Today, many people want to abolish blood sports.
   4 Blood sport supporters are determined keep blood sports.
   5 ... fox-hunting can be an important event, a time when people meet and enjoy themselves together.
G cruelty, terror, painfully, suffering

7 Blood sports (continued)

B Read the paragraphs in the correct order. Then, in pairs, answer these questions.

1. Which paragraph gives the arguments against blood sports? Which paragraph gives the arguments in favour of blood sports?
2. Summarize in writing the arguments against blood sports. Then summarize the arguments in favour of blood sports.
3. How do you think the author of this essay feels about blood sports? Or can't you say?

C Find these words in the text. Choose the word or phrase below which best explains them.

1. *eager* (paragraph b) **a** wanting to do something very much **b** happy
2. *to abolish* (paragraph e) **a** to change **b** to stop
3. *campaigner* (paragraph d) **a** someone who tries to change something **b** an angry person
4. *to march* (paragraph d) **a** to walk with others in protest against something **b** to walk a long way

D Match the sport with the description below.

a bullfighting   **b** cockfighting   **c** fox-hunting

1. Two animals are made to fight. They wear metal spikes on their legs.
2. An animal is chased and killed by dogs.
3. An animal is attacked and finally killed with thin spears.

E Explain the meaning of the underlined words.

1. Certainly, for thousands of years man hunted from necessity.
2. In Britain it has brought people out on the streets.
3. Today, many people want to abolish such practices.
4. Blood sport supporters are determined to fight back.
5. For country people in Britain, fox-hunting can be an important social occasion.

F Answer these questions.

1. Are there blood sports in your country? How do people feel about them?
2. The end of the text reads: 'Who will succeed in the end? At present it is impossible to say.' Do you agree with this statement? Or do you think the anti-blood-sport campaigners will win and blood sports will be abolished? If so, when do you think this will happen? Give reasons for your opinion.
3. How do you feel about blood sports? Give reasons for your opinion.

G Look at the text again and find four negative words associated with blood sports.

Teacher's notes

8 Self-awareness

Aim	To understand an account of a new scientific discovery.
Preparation	Copy the handouts on pages 35, 37 and 39 – one copy per student.

Introduction (5 minutes)

Activity A Ask students to look at the pictures in Activity A. Ask them for the names of the animals in the pictures (*chimpanzee, tiger* and *dolphin*). Point to the question above the pictures and ask: *Which of these creatures is self-aware?* Elicit/teach the meaning of *creature, self-aware (self-aware = aware that you exist, that you are a person)*. Elicit answers from students but do not stay too long on their answers as the subject will be explored in this lesson.

Presentation (15 minutes)

Activity B In small groups, students read the statements and mark them with a tick or a cross, according to whether they agree or disagree with them. They use their dictionaries where necessary. Check that students understand the statements by asking questions. Encourage discussion and correct major errors. Students can continue the discussion in groups, if wished. Example language: *I agree with statement 1. No animals are self-aware. I disagree with statement 6. Animals can be very loving. Look at dolphins, for example. There are many stories about them helping people.*

(continued on page 36)

8 Self-awareness

A Which of these creatures are self-aware?

B Work in small groups. Read these statements. Tick (✔) the statements you agree with. Put a cross (✘) by the statements you disagree with. Explain why you agree or disagree with the statements.

1 Humans have self-awareness. No animals have this.

2 Humans feel emotions such as happiness and sadness. Animals do not have real feelings.

3 Humans play in a way that animals do not.

4 Humans are creative. Animals are not.

5 Humans can be cruel. Animals are never cruel.

6 Humans can be very kind and loving. Animals love their young but this is just an instinct.

7 Humans have far greater intelligence than animals.

From *Instant Lessons 2 Intermediate* edited by Peter Watcyn-Jones © Penguin Books 2000

Teacher's notes

Practice *(30 minutes)*

Activity C In pairs, students read the text and choose the right answers from the questions below. Pre-teach the word *cell* (= *the smallest part of an animal or plant that can exist on its own*). If you wish, pre-teach key vocabulary: *cell, integrate, evidence, discovery, to injure, mentally ill, depressed, senile, species*. Alternatively, students can use their dictionaries. Check answers orally, explaining where necessary.

(continued on page 38)

Key

C 1a 2b 3a 4b

(continued on page 38)

8 Self-awareness (continued)

C Work in pairs. Read the following and then choose the correct answer, a or b.

Scientists in California, America, have found the cells in the brain that make humans self-aware. The cells are large and lie in the front part of the brain, near the centre. The cells integrate the work of the various parts of the brain. They give us the sense that we are a person, the feeling that we exist.

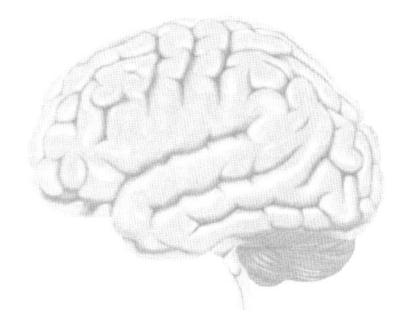

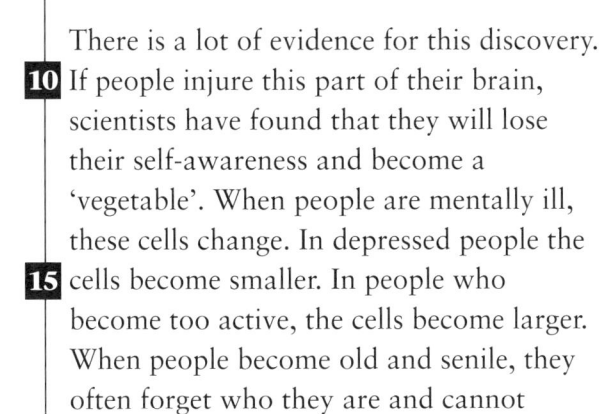

There is a lot of evidence for this discovery. If people injure this part of their brain, scientists have found that they will lose their self-awareness and become a 'vegetable'. When people are mentally ill, these cells change. In depressed people the cells become smaller. In people who become too active, the cells become larger. When people become old and senile, they often forget who they are and cannot recognize their family. In such cases, the cells disappear completely.

The Californian scientists looked for the same cells in the brains of 48 animal species. They found that chimpanzees have these cells, but do not have as many as humans. Gorillas have these cells too, but they have fewer of them than chimpanzees.

The human brain

1 These 'self-awareness' cells:
   a give us the feeling that we are a person.
   b are found in different parts of the brain.

2 These cells can become smaller when:
   a someone damages this part of their brain.
   b someone is mentally ill.

3 When people become senile, these cells can:
   a disappear.
   b make people forget who they are.

4 The scientists found that:
   a gorillas have more of these cells than chimpanzees.
   b chimpanzees have more of these cells than gorillas.

Teacher's notes

Activity D In pairs, students write answers to the questions, using their dictionaries. Walk round and check what students have written. Also check answers orally, explaining where necessary. Write example answers on the board.

Activity E Students can discuss these questions in small groups. Walk round and correct major errors. Then have a whole class discussion on the questions. Write up corrections of key mistakes on the board. Question 3: Note that scientists suspect that elephants and dolphins may have these 'self-awareness' cells too. Write new words on the board in sentences.

Conclusion (5 minutes)

Activity F Walk round and check what students have written.

Homework

Written answers to Activity E.

Key

D 1 a disappear
    b various
    c integrate
    d emotions
    e lie
    f depressed
    g senile
  2 We mean that the person is physically alive but can hardly think or move. This can happen because of illness or injury.
  3 You could break your leg or cut it. You could injure it when you are skiing, or if something heavy falls on it.
  4 Art – for example, music, painting, writing. Buildings, science.
  5 We have discovered their bones.

E 1 *Open answer*
  2 *Open answer*
  3 Scientists suspect that elephants and dolphins may have these 'self-awareness' cells too.
  4 *Open answer*

8 Self-awareness (continued)

D Work in pairs. Write answers to these questions.

1 Find words in the texts in Activities B and C that mean the same as these words:
   a vanish (d...)
   b different (v...)
   c to make things work together (i...)
   d feelings (e...)
   e are found (l...)
   f sad and without a love of life (d...)
   g mentally confused because of old age (s...)

2 What do we mean when we say that someone is a vegetable?

3 How could you injure your leg?

4 Give three examples of human creativity.

5 What evidence is there that dinosaurs existed?

E Work in small groups. Discuss the questions.

1 Does the text in Activity C surprise you? Say why/why not.

2 Go back to Activity B. Is there any statement you have changed your mind about?

3 Do you think that there are any other animals that might have these 'self-awareness' cells in the brain? Give reasons for your opinion.

4 Now that you know that chimpanzees and gorillas have these cells, do you think we should treat them differently? For example, should we put them in zoos? Give reasons for your opinion.

F Complete one of these sentences.

1 I think we should treat animals such as chimpanzees and gorillas differently because ...

2 I don't think we should treat these animals differently because ...

Teacher's notes

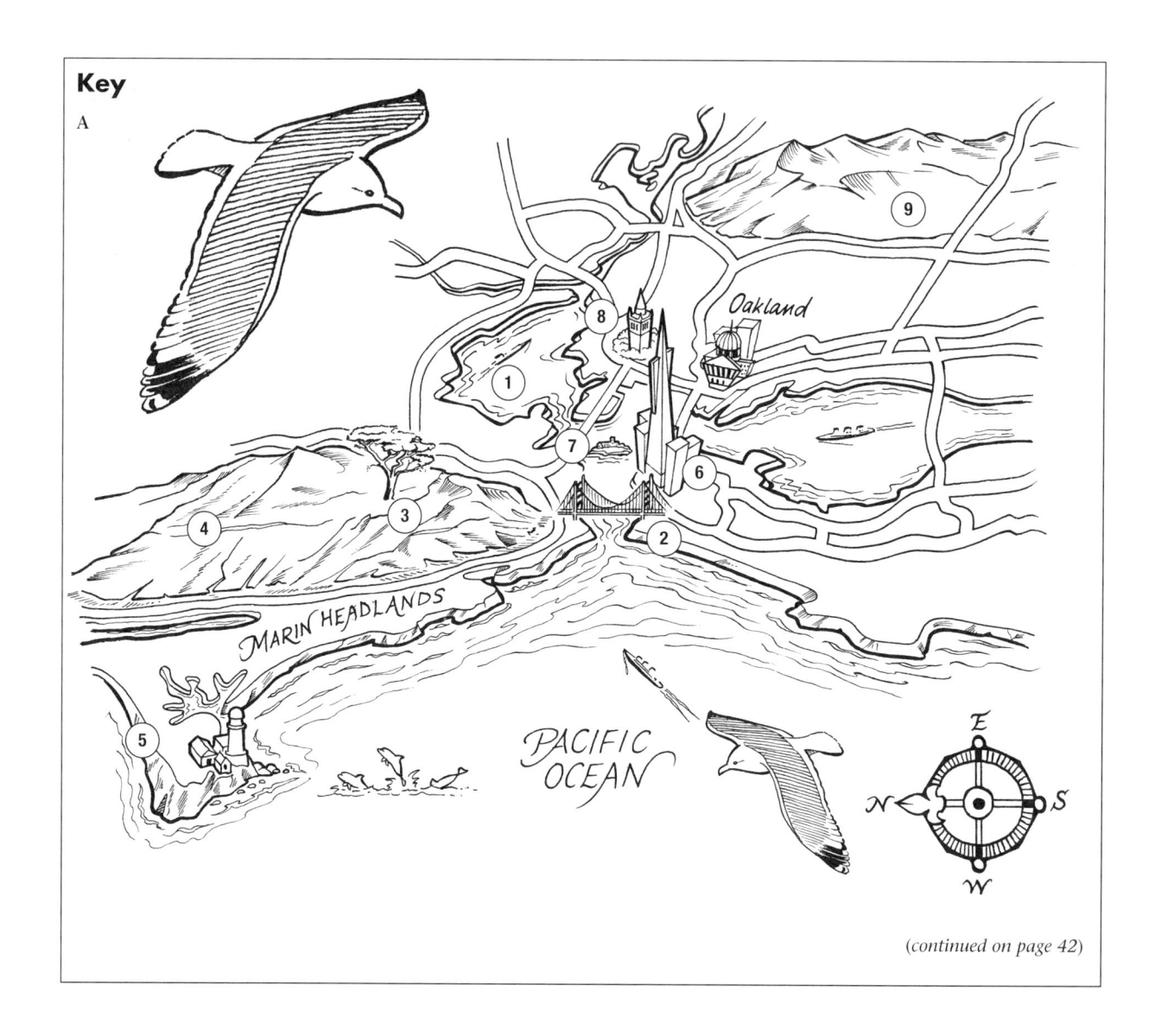

9 San Francisco

Aim	To read a description of a geographical area and identify places on a map.
Preparation	Copy the handouts on pages 41, 43 and 45 – one copy per student.

Introduction (5 minutes)

Students look at the map. Ask them: *What do you know about San Francisco?* Elicit answers. You may find students need these words: *west coast, bay, Pacific Ocean, Golden Gate Bridge*.

Presentation (15 minutes)

Activity A In pairs, students look at the map and read the text. They write the right numbers in the white circles on the map. Allow them to use dictionaries. Alternatively, you may wish to pre-teach key vocabulary: *tip, peninsula, bay, coast, to connect, abundance, wildlife, situated, range*. Walk round, giving help and encouragement. Check answers orally, explaining where necessary.

(continued on page 42)

Key
A

(continued on page 42)

9 San Francisco

A Look at the map and read the text. Put the right numbers in the circles on the map.

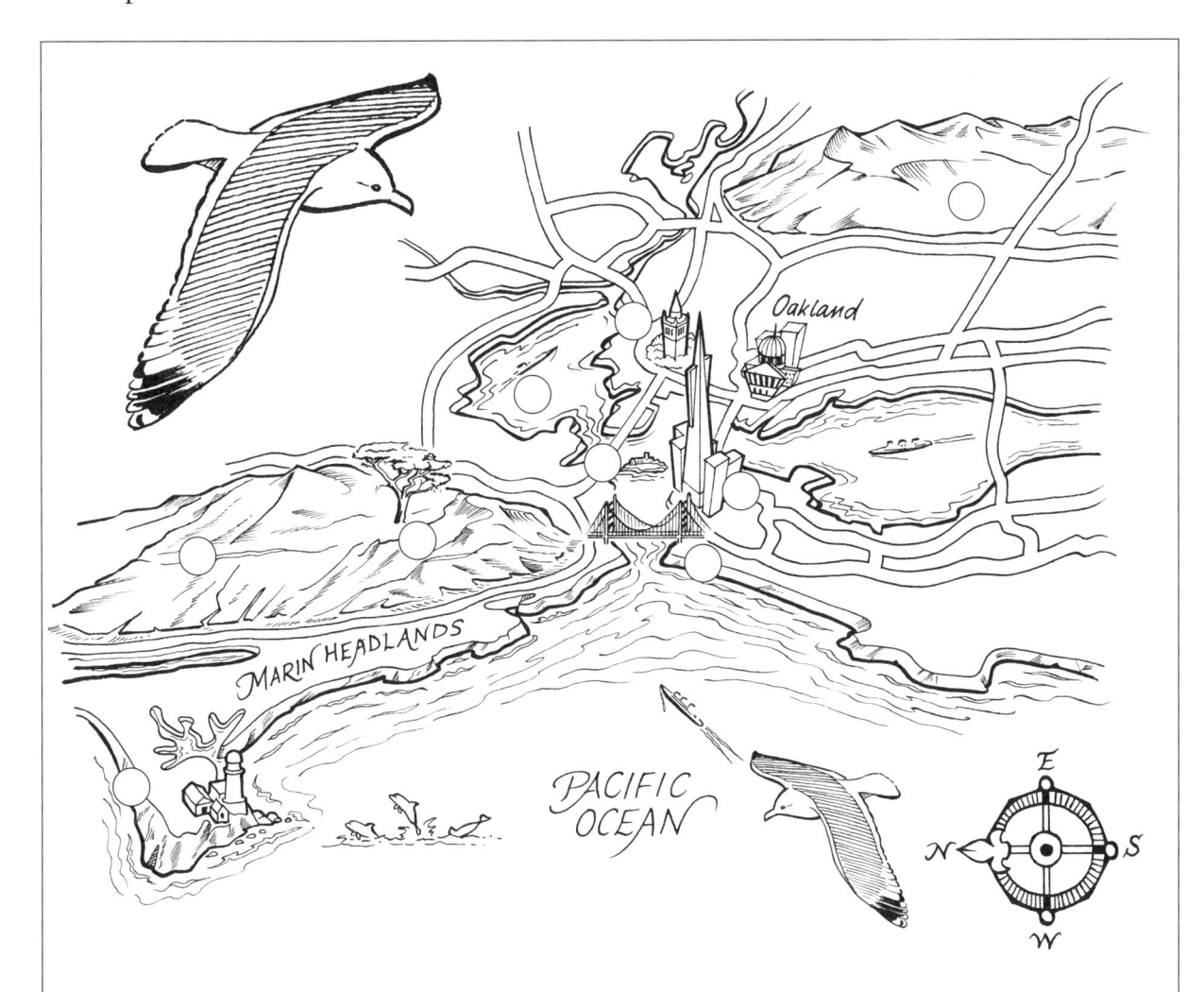

San Francisco City, with its 43 hills, lies at the tip of a peninsula on the western coast of America. To the west is the Pacific Ocean. To the east is (1) San Francisco Bay. A famous bridge, (2) the Golden Gate Bridge, connects the city with the Marin Headlands. These green hills and quiet beaches mean that San Franciscans can get away from the noise of the city and be in the hills or by the sea in under an hour. A short way along this coast one finds (3) the Muir Woods. As you go further north you reach (4) the Sonoma Mountains. Going west from there, you come to (5) Point Reyes Peninsula, an area known for its abundance of wildlife.

The tallest building in San Francisco, (6) the Transamerica Pyramid, is situated in the northeast of the city. There is a small island in the bay itself, three miles east of Golden Gate Bridge. This is the famous island prison (7) Alcatraz. A second bridge, Bay Bridge, runs across the bay to Oakland, which has one of the busiest ports in the USA. Just north of Oakland is the city of (8) Berkeley, famous for the University of California. East of Berkeley and Oakland lies (9) the Diablo Coast Range, with mountains reaching up to 1173 metres.

From *Instant Lessons 2 Intermediate* edited by Peter Watcyn-Jones © Penguin Books 2000

Teacher's notes

Activity B In pairs, students read the sentences and write the right number for each. They use their dictionaries. Walk round and check what students have written. Also check answers orally. Write new words on the board in sentences.

Practice *(25 minutes)*

Activity C In pairs, students answer the questions. Check answers orally. For questions 2, 3 and 4, be ready to help students with vocabulary (see key). Encourage students to use their dictionaries.

(continued on page 44)

Key

B a7 b9 c3 d5 e6 f2
C 1 *Open answer*
   2 *Possible answers:* seals, sea otters, eagles, whales
   3 *Possible answers:* the Himalayas, the Alps, the Pyrenees, the Andes
   4 *Possible answer:* sparrows, pigeons, parrots, eagles
   5 Three
   6 *Open answer*

(continued on page 44)

9 San Francisco (continued)

B Work in pairs. Read these sentences. They tell you more about the places described above. Write the right numbers beside the sentences.

a Notorious 1930s gangster Al Capone spent five years here.

....

b Some of the greatest scientists in the world are employed here.

....

c This forest has redwood trees in it that are over 1000 years old.

....

d This area has 360 species of birds.

....

e This building reaches 360 metres above sea level and was disliked by San Franciscans when it opened in 1972.

....

f This bridge, which connects San Francisco with the Pacific coast, cost $35 million to build and was opened in 1937.

....

C Work in pairs. Answer these questions.
1 Do you live by the sea or do you live inland? If you don't live by the sea, would you like to? Say why/why not.
2 What wildlife do you think you might see on the Pacific coast of America?
3 Name a famous mountain range in either Asia, Europe or South America.
4 Name one species of bird.
5 How many sides of a peninsula are surrounded by the sea?
6 Which place in Activities A and B would you most like to visit? Say why.

Teacher's notes

Activity D Students read the text and underline the wrongly used words. They use their dictionaries. Students also try and guess what the right words are. Check answers orally, explaining where necessary.

Activty E In pairs, students complete these sentences. Check what students have written. Also check answers orally and write model answers on the board. Write new words on the board in sentences.

Activity F Students discuss these questions in small groups. Then have a whole class disucssion on the subject. Correct major errors.

Conclusion (5 minutes)

Students write two sentences describing San Francisco without looking at the handouts. Walk round and check what they have written.

Homework

Written answers to Activity F.

Key

D ... Being an inland (coastal) city ... making circles (squares) as they do in many American cities ... the centre of the countryside (city) quite fast ... the meat (seafood) is first class ... San Franciscans talk about the weather (food) a lot ... you must avoid (visit) if you can.

E 1 ... of the sea breezes.
2 ... they are straight.
3 ... they are fun to ride and get you round the centre of the city quite fast.
4 ... it is a coastal city.
5 ... San Francisco has an enormous population of Chinese and Latin Americans.
6 ... it's a fine, delightful city.

9 San Francisco (continued)

D Work in pairs. Read this text. There are six words used wrongly. Find them and underline them. Think of suitable words to put in their place.

Many people would list San Francisco as one of the most delightful cities in the world. Being an inland city, there's a feeling of the sea in the air; the sea breezes wake you up, make you eat well and sleep well. The city was planned with straight roads, and these roads cross each other at right angles, making circles as they do in many American cities. Very often you can find yourself on top of a hill in the city, looking down one of these straight roads as it rises and falls on its journey through the town. It's a beautiful sight. A good way to travel these roads is by cable car. These are buses that run on rails in the ground up and down the steep hills. There are only three lines but they are fun to ride and get you round the centre of the countryside quite fast.

The food is delicious in San Francisco. This is because of two things. Firstly, being on the coast, the meat is first class – there are prawns as big as a man's hand. Secondly, San Francisco has an enormous population of Chinese and Latin Americans. Consequently, there is a multicultural flavour to the cooking. San Franciscans talk about the weather a lot! All in all, San Francisco – or SF, as those who live there call it – is a fine city, one you must avoid if you can.

E Work in pairs. Complete these sentences in writing.

1 You sleep well in San Francisco because ...
2 You can see down the roads in San Francisco because ...
3 You should travel by cable car in San Francisco because ...
4 The seafood is good in San Francisco because ...
5 You can eat many different kinds of cuisine in San Francisco because ...
6 You should visit San Francisco because ...

F Work in small groups. Discuss these questions.

1 Have you ever been to the USA?
2 If so, where? What was it like?
3 If not, where would you like to go to and why?

Teacher's notes

10 Recipes

Aim	To understand and complete cooking instructions.
Preparation	Copy the handouts on pages 47 and 49 – one copy per student.

Introduction *(5–10 minutes)*

Ask students these questions: *Do you cook? How often? Do you enjoy cooking? When you cook, do you follow recipes?* Students can then ask and answer in pairs. Example language: *Do you use recipes? I've learnt to cook some things. But I often use recipes.*

Presentation *(15–20 minutes)*

Activity A Students look at picture a and answer question 1. Elicit/teach: *slice, leek*. Then students read questions 2 and 3. Elicit/teach the word *joke*. They read the recipes and answer questions 2 and 3, without using dictionaries if possible. Check answers orally, explaining where necessary. Question 3: Example of language to explain the joke: *You don't need a recipe for a glass of water. You just go to the tap and turn it on!*

Activity B Check students understand the questions. Then they read the two recipes again. Encourage them to use their dictionaries if necessary, but not for every word. Then check orally, explaining where necessary. Write new words on the board in sentences.

(continued on page 48)

Key

A 1 Someone is slicing leeks.
   2 Recipe 1: the picture of the glass of water. Recipe 2: the picture of someone slicing leeks.
   3 Recipe 1 is a joke. You don't need a recipe to pour a glass of water. Perhaps the writer is making a joke about cookery writers. Sometimes they explain how to cook very simple things.

B 1a ... pour a glass of cold water.
   1b ... make leek and potato soup.
   2 oil, vegetable stock, cream
   3 salt and pepper
   4 *Open answer*

(continued on page 48)

10 Recipes

A Answer these questions.

1 What is happening in picture a?

2 Read these two recipes. Then match them with the pictures.

3 Which one of these two recipes is a joke? Explain why.

a

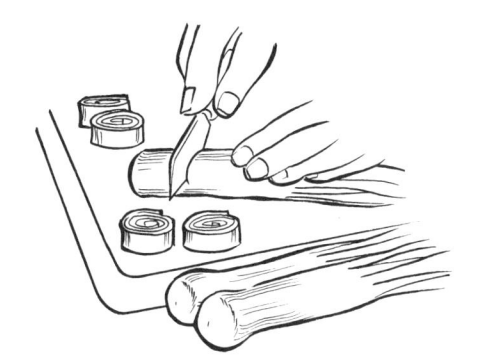

b

1

- Take one glass of water (made out of glass and without any holes in it, if possible) and place under the tap. Cold water is better than hot.
- Let the cold tap (marked 'C') run for a few seconds before filling the glass.
- Don't forget to turn off the tap when the glass is full – but don't turn it off too soon or you won't have any water.
- With practice, you'll learn to do it and you'll have a delicious glass of water. Serves one.

2

4 leeks
40ml oil
1 litre vegetable stock
salt and pepper
1 onion
350g potatoes
200ml cream

- Slice the leeks and onions. Heat the oil in a saucepan, add the leeks and onion and cook gently for about ten minutes.
- Thinly slice the potatoes and add to the pan with the stock. When it is boiling, lower the heat. Simmer for thirty minutes.
- Puree the soup in a food processor. Stir in cream and serve.

B Now answer these questions.

1 Complete these sentences.

a Recipe 1 tells you how to ...

b Recipe 2 tell you how to ...

2 Which of the ingredients in recipe 2 are liquids?

3 Which ingredients are not in the instructions on how to make the soup?

4 Do you eat this soup or something like it in your country?

From *Instant Lessons 2 Intermediate* edited by Peter Watcyn-Jones © Penguin Books 2000

Teacher's notes

Practice (20 minutes)

Activity C Question 1: In pairs, students go through recipe 2, underlining the cooking verbs.
Encourage them to guess the meaning. If they can't, explain. Then check orally, explaining where necessary. Then students write the verbs down and translate them. For questions 2 and 3, use the pictures to teach vocabulary: *courgette, pepper, strip, wok, fry*.

Activity D Go through the ingredients in the list, checking students understand them. Note: *Soy sauce* is a Japanese sauce. *Sherry* is a pale or dark brown strong wine. Check students understand the questions. Then they read the recipe and answer the questions, using dictionaries where necessary. Then check answers orally, explaining where necessary. Write new words on the board in sentences.

Optional Extension In pairs, students explain how to fry potatoes. Ask: *How do you fry potatoes?* Example language: *Peel the potatoes and boil them for five minutes. Then thinly slice them. Heat some oil in a frying pan. When the oil is hot, put the potatoes in the pan. Fry them for four minutes each side.*

Conclusion (5 minutes)

Activity E Example answer: *I know how to cook steak and chips.* Use dictionaries if necessary.

Homework

Ask students to find a recipe. They can choose from: a favourite recipe, one typical of their country/region, one they've tried and liked, one they've never tried but would like to try, one they found interesting or different, etc. Ask students to write the recipe in English and bring the recipe to the next lesson.

Key

C 1 slice, heat, add, cook, boil, lower the heat, simmer, puree, stir, serve
   2 courgettes, (red) peppers, chicken
   3 It was fried.

D 1 Paragraph 1/Picture c
      Paragraph 2/Picture a
      Paragraph 3/Picture b
   2 1 Slice 2 Slice 3 Heat 4 Add 5 Add 6 Stir 7 Serve

10 Recipes *(continued)*

C Now answer these questions.

1. Which words in recipe 2 are cooking verbs? Write them down and translate them.
2. Look at the three pictures below. What food can you see?
3. In picture b, how do you think the food was cooked?

a   b   c

D Read the recipe below.

1. Match the pictures with the paragraphs.
2. Use some of the cooking verbs from recipe 2 to complete the sentences.

| 450g courgettes | 30ml oil | 15ml soy sauce | 1 red pepper |

| 1 garlic clove pepper | 450g chicken breasts | 45ml dry sherry |

1 (1) .... the courgettes and peppers into long thin strips.

2 (2) .... the chicken into thin strips. (3) .... the oil in a large frying pan or wok and fry the garlic for one minute. (4) .... the chicken and cook for three or four minutes, stirring continuously.

3 (5) .... the courgettes and pepper and continue to cook for two minutes, until the chicken is cooked and the vegetables are tender but crisp. (6) .... in the sherry and soy sauce and cook for one minute. Add salt and pepper. (7) .... with boiled rice.

E What do you know how to cook? Name three things.

Writing: Lessons 11–20

11 Are you green?

Aim	To activate vocabulary connected with the environment and green issues by completing the writing of a questionnaire and answering a letter.
Preparation	Copy the handout on page 51 – one copy per student.

Introduction *(5 minutes)*

Introduce the subject of conservation/ecology by saying that today you are green! Give a few examples of what you have done, for example: *bought some recycled paper, cycled to school*, etc. to help them to work out what this means. Then brainstorm for vocabulary on the topic, writing all the words and expressions on the board; for example: *waste, recycle, energy, resources*, etc. Then write up the question:
How green are you?
and the answers:
I'm very green – I ...
I'm not very green – I ... / I don't ...
Students work briefly with a partner to ask each other the question. Listen to some of the answers as a class.

Presentation and Practice 1 *(30 minutes)*

Give each student a copy of the questionnaire. Explain that this is going to be put in a magazine to see how green the readers are, but the journalist writing it has had to go out on a big scoop and the deadline is fast approaching! They are going to work together in small groups to finish it off and test it on one another. Point out that the questions need finishing as well as the scoring system and the score comments. Read through question 1 as an example, pointing out the structure, i.e. a situation followed by a question followed by three possible answers. Work as a class to give each answer points – 5 for the best answer, 3 for the next best and 1 for the worst.
Divide the class into small groups (between three and five students) and try to mix the abilities so that the more able can help the others. Their task is now to complete the questionnaire and its scoring, discussing it together and then filling in their own sheet. While they work, circulate to help with any problems. If necessary, allow students to add a fourth category: *none of these*.

Once the questionnaires are ready, pair students up with someone from another group so that they can ask each other the questions and note down the scores.
End this part of the activity with a whole class round-up to see who are the greenest students – and, perhaps, the least green!

Practice 2 *(10 minutes)*

Present the following letter to the class either by reading it as a dictation, by writing it up on the board or by using an overhead projector.
Dear Green Magazine,
I want to help the environment but I don't know how. I'm fifteen and I live in a flat in a big city so I can't cycle to school or grow vegetables. I don't have a car, go shopping or have much money. So what can I do?
A worried student
Give them 5 minutes to write a short reply working individually. When they have finished, put them into groups to read one another's letters and choose the best. The ones chosen by each group are read out to the whole class.

Conclusion *(5 minutes)*

Working as a class, try to decide on the three most important actions the students can take to help their own immediate environment. You might end by asking how many ways they could use/re-use the photocopied questionnaire!

Homework

Students could expand and write up their reply from Practice 2, or they could write a short questionnaire for you to fill in.

11 Are you green?

Here is a questionnaire to find out!

1. You like magazines and read two or three a week. What do you do with your old magazines?
   - (1) Give them to your friends to read.
   - (2) Burn them in the garden.
   - (3) Take them to the paper bank to be recycled.

2. You buy food at your local shop. How do you carry it home?
   - (1) Ask the shop for a cardboard box to carry it in.
   - (2) Ask the shop to deliver it.
   - (3) Bring your own bag with you.

3. You have bought some smart new clothes. What do you do with the old clothes that you don't wear any more?
   - (1) Sell them and buy more clothes with the money.
   - (2) Give them to a charity like the Red Cross, or to the church.
   - (3) _____

4. You live 5km from the place where you work or study. How do you get there each day?
   - (1) Cycle.
   - (2) Go in a friend's car to save petrol.
   - (3) _____

5. You've just spent a lovely day having a picnic on the beach. What do you do with the food you haven't eaten?
   - (1) Throw it in the sea for the birds and fish to eat.
   - (2) _____
   - (3) _____

6. _____
   - (1) _____
   - (2) _____
   - (3) _____

ANSWERS

1 (1) =   (2) =   (3) =
2 (1) =   (2) =   (3) =
3 (1) =   (2) =   (3) =
4 (1) =   (2) =   (3) =
5 (1) =   (2) =   (3) =
6 (1) =   (2) =   (3) =

SCORES

- **0–10** OH NO! You are not very green! Think about what you can do to be better.
- **10–20** NOT BAD! You are quite green!
- **20–30** GREAT!

Teacher's notes

12 My CV

Aim	To write a simple curriculum vitae, following a standard format.
Preparation	Copy the handout on page 53 – two copies per student.

Introduction (5 minutes)

Introduce the topic of CVs by saying that a friend of yours has just applied for a job and that you have been helping him/her to write a CV. Explain what this means and ask the class to jot down ten pieces of information that should go in a typical one (see handout for ideas). Write these on the board and make sure everyone understands them.

Presentation (15 minutes)

Give everyone a copy of the handout and go through the different sections. Then say that you are going to tell them about someone you know and as you speak they should write the relevant information in the correct spaces (on the first handout only). Speak slowly and spell any proper names.
Bob – that's short for Robert – Robert John Adams – is British although he now lives in the USA in Los Angeles – at 1084 Franklin Avenue to be precise. He's married to a friend of mine and he teaches International Law at the Central College for Legal Studies. Before that he worked as a legal adviser for a big international company in London for five years. He studied Law at the University of Oxford and has a BA in Law and a Diploma in International Law. Before that he was at school in Birmingham at St Martin's School for Boys where he did very well, passing four subjects at Advanced level – English, Spanish, History and Economics. He's a very keen cyclist, has a black belt in judo and he and I are both very interested in computers and keeping fit. I have to ring him tonight on 213 851 0890 to wish him a happy birthday – he's 32 today!
Repeat if necessary and then put students into pairs and let them compare their work. Briefly note the correct answers on the board (nothing was said about referees but presumably you would be one for him as you know him so well!) Note vocabulary for qualifications (*Advanced level/A level, diploma, degree*, etc.)

Practice (25 minutes)

So now the class know how to put together a CV, ask them what sort of jobs it would be interesting to apply for and put a list of suggestions on the board. Encourage some interesting and unusual positions, for example: *president of a small country / star of a new Hollywood blockbuster / guide for a round-the-world trip / English teacher to a royal family / head of their school / interpreter for the American president / television news reporter / fashion designer / leader of an expedition to the South Pole*, etc. Divide class into groups of four or five students and let each group choose a job to apply for. Give each student another copy of the handout. Allow 5 minutes for everyone to work individually to write a CV for their job. They can include some of their own details and invent others, or they can write a purely imaginary CV. (Explain that names must remain in their own language and that qualifications will need some kind of English explanation.) Students now work in groups and read one another's CV, choosing the best person for their particular job. Successful candidates read out their CV to the class for comment.

Conclusion (5 minutes)

Discuss what makes a good CV and what else is important, for example an interview. Are there things that should not be included in a CV, for example personal details?

Homework

They write a CV or a short account of the career of someone they know.

Key

Name: Robert John Adams
Address: 1084 Franklin Avenue, Los Angeles, USA
Telephone number: 213 851 0890
Date of birth: Exactly 32 years from the date of the lesson
Nationality: British
Marital status: Married
Education: St Martin's School for Boys, Birmingham; University of Oxford
Qualifications: A levels in English, Spanish, History and Economics; BA in Law; Diploma in International Law
Present position: Teacher of International Law at Central College for Legal Studies
Previous employment: Legal adviser for international company in London for five years
Additional skills and interests: cycling, judo (black belt), computers, keeping fit

12 My CV

Curriculum Vitae

Name: ....

Address: ....

....

Telephone number: ....

Date of birth: ....

Nationality: ....

Marital status: ....

Education: ....

....

....

Qualifications: ....

....

....

Present position: ....

Previous employment: ....

....

....

Additional skills and interests: ....

....

....

Referees: ....

....

Teacher's notes

13 Writing home

Aim	To practise writing postcards/short letters from a variety of places.
Preparation	Copy and cut up the handout on page 55 – one copy per pair or group of three. Bring in a holiday postcard you have received.

Introduction (5 minutes)

Bring in a holiday postcard you have received and read it to the class. Invite them to guess where it is from. Ask if they like receiving and sending postcards and what sort of information is usually given on them: what the person has been doing, the weather, future plans, hello to those back home, etc. Draw attention to the way a postcard is usually set out, with the message on the left and the address on the right.

Presentation (20 minutes)

Divide the class into pairs or groups of three and give each pair/group a copy of the handout cut up into twenty slips of paper.
Explain that two holiday postcards have been torn up and mixed up. Their task is to reconstruct the two cards correctly, using clues in the text and their knowledge of postcard layout. Each postcard has ten different pieces. The first pair/group to finish wins. Wait until several groups have finished before inviting them to read out the correct solutions. Note the vocabulary and style: short sentences, typical beginning and close, etc.

Practice (20 minutes)

Ask the class to suggest interesting places to go on holiday (money no object) and write a list on the board. For example: *the Moon, the North Pole, the Olympics, a space station, a submarine, a jungle, a safari, a carnival, an expedition*, etc. Put them back into their previous pairs/groups and ask them to write a postcard home from one of these places (or another place of their own choosing), giving details about what they have been doing but not mentioning the place by name. Allow about 10 minutes for this, circulating to help with vocabulary if necessary. Then each pair/group reads out the postcard and the rest of the class guess where it is from. While this is going on, make a note of any mistakes and then discuss these briefly on the board afterwards.

Conclusion (5 minutes)

Launch the shortest postcard competition! In some countries, postage is cheaper if fewer than five words are written on a card as the message. Give 2 minutes for thought and then ask for ideas. The most pithy and interesting deserve a round of applause.

Homework

A dream holiday has not turned out as planned. Write an appropriate postcard home.

Key

Hi Carlos!
New York is great! We saw the Statue of Liberty yesterday morning
and went to Central Park in the afternoon. In the evening
we had enormous hamburgers and French fries. I've now got an
American accent – you'll be able to hear it when I get home.
Lots of love, Anna

Carlos Mendez
Calle Menorca 5
Madrid
Spain

Dear Julie and Alan,
This year we are in Nice in the south of France and the weather is
fantastic. We go swimming every day and then to restaurants and
discos at night. It's wonderful to dance under the stars!
How was your holiday swimming round the Great Barrier Reef?
See you soon. Jamie and Sarah

Julie and Alan Webb
8 Beal Street
Sydney
New South Wales
Australia

13 Writing home

Dear Julie and Alan, This year we are in Nice,	Julie and Alan Webb
in the south of France and the weather is fantastic.	8 Beal Street
We go swimming every day and then go to restaurants	Sydney
and discos at night. It's wonderful to dance under the stars!	New South Wales
How was you holiday swimming round the Great Barrier Reef? See you soon. Jamie and Sarah	Australia
Hi Carlos! New York is great!	Carlos Mendez
We saw the Statue of Liberty yesterday morning	Calle Menorca 5
and went to Central Park in the afternoon.	Madrid
In the evening we had enormous hamburgers and french fries.	Spain
I've now got an American accent —	you'll be able to hear it when I get home. Lots of love, Anna

From *Instant Lessons 2 Intermediate* edited by Peter Watcyn-Jones © Penguin Books 2000

Teacher's notes

14 A warm welcome

Aim	To introduce vocabulary for hotel facilities and to practise writing a letter to reserve hotel accommodation.
Preparation	Copy and cut up the handout on page 57 – one copy per student.

Introduction (5 minutes)

Introduce the topic by saying that you are planning to spend a few nights in a hotel and have received details. Now you have to decide what sort of hotel and room you want. Write the letters
S D T F
on the board and ask the class to guess what sort of rooms they refer to (*Single, Double, Twin, Family*). Then add an *e* to each letter, so you have:
Se De Te Fe
and ask for suggestions. (*e = en suite*, meaning that there is a private bathroom attached to the room.)

Presentation (15 minutes)

Activity A Give students a copy of the symbols. Explain that these are standard symbols to give details of what facilities are available. Divide the class into small groups (four students maximum) and ask them to write down what they think each symbol means. When they have done all they can, give them the rest of the handout. They should look at the list and use this to help them complete their work. Those who finish early should choose the five facilities they consider most important and also any they do not consider useful. Go through the answers checking that everyone understands, and discuss facilities.

Practice (25 minutes)

Activity B Read through the details of the Swan Hotel and explain that each group is now going to write a letter to this hotel to book some rooms for a short break.

Check first that they know how to set out a formal letter and if necessary do a model on the board. Then discuss what information they need to give the hotel: number of adults and children, number and type of rooms, length of stay, dates, time of arrival and departure, meals required, car parking, etc. Also discuss any requests: special diets, animals, disabled access, facilities for children, price, special rates, payment, etc. Ask each group to note down some details on a piece of paper, for example:
A stay of two nights for a couple and a six-year-old child, Saturday 7 February and Sunday 8 February. Bed, breakfast and dinner. All vegetarians. Would like to bring their dog. Would like to know the rate for the child and the total cost.
The information they write down will be given to another group who will then write the letter to the Swan Hotel. Give a few minutes for groups to make their list and then collect and redistribute. Students at first work individually to write the letter and then read what the others in their group have written. Taking the best from each one, they write a final letter all together which is read aloud.

Conclusion (5 minutes)

Activity C Draw students' attention to the text about Jennifer and Barney Wainwright, at the bottom of the page. Ask them, in pairs, to work out the Wainwrights' bill, referring to the tariff of the Swan Hotel.

Homework

Students can write a personal letter to a hotel to book a room.

Key
C £288.50

14 A warm welcome

A Hotels and Guest Houses

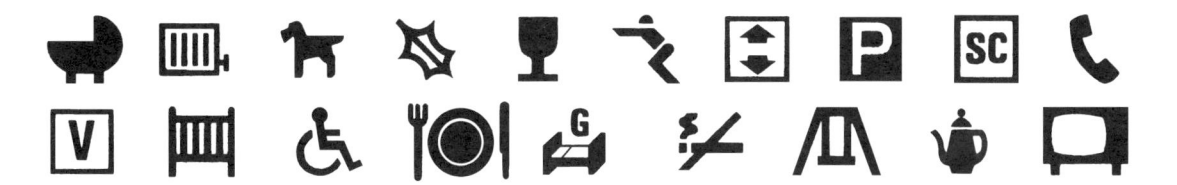

- Private parking • Dogs by arrangement • Special rates for children •
- Licensed club or bar • Cot provided • Central heating • Heated pool •
- Special Christmas/New Year package • Non-smoking establishment • Lift •
- TV in rooms • Tea/coffee facilities in rooms • Evening meals available •
- Vegetarian diets • Ground floor rooms • Babysitting service •
- Children's play area • Facilities for disabled • Telephone in rooms •

B

THE SWAN HOTEL

A 17th-century hotel fully restored with comfort, style and all modern conveniences. Perfectly situated with picturesque views of the surrounding countryside. First class service in a friendly atmosphere with superb award-winning restaurant. Ideal centre for visiting the area.

OPEN ALL YEAR

	Low Season Bed and breakfast	Low Season Dinner, bed and breakfast	High Season Bed and breakfast	High Season Dinner, bed and breakfast
Midweek	£29.50	£37.00	£35.50	£42.00
Weekend	£39.50	£47.00	£45.50	£52.00

All double rooms have a private bathroom en suite, colour TV and tea making facilities.
All guests have the use of the two sitting rooms and dining room.
Prices are per person on a double occupancy basis and include service, a full English breakfast and VAT.
Low Season: January, February, March, November and December (special rates apply for Christmas and New Year)
Midweek: Sunday to Thursday inclusive
Afternoon Tea: £4.75

The Swan Hotel
Sherborne Dorset
☎: 01849 294301

C Jennifer and Barney Wainwright stay three nights at the Swan Hotel, bed and breakfast, arriving on Thursday 12 April at 6pm and leaving on Sunday 15 April after breakfast. They have dinner on Thursday and Saturday and afternoon tea on Friday. What is their total bill?

Teacher's notes

15 Where to go and what to see

Aim	To practise writing simple tourist literature describing the attractions of the area.
Preparation	Copy the handout on page 59 – one copy per student.
(Optional)	Bring in some English tourist brochures as examples.

Introduction *(10 minutes)*

Tell the class that some friends of yours are coming to visit and ask for suggestions as to where to take them both in the town and in the surrounding area. List these on the board, trying to get at least a dozen places and making sure that students know the English words for each one, for example: *museum, old house, park, church*, etc. Introduce the subject of tourism and tourist literature by asking about tourists to the area and where they could get information.

Presentation and Practice 1 *(25 minutes)*

Give out the handouts and explain that you are going to look at tourist information about a city in England called Rochester. Show its position on the map and give students a few minutes to read the information before asking them to turn the handouts over and note down Rochester's main attractions (six mentioned by name plus shops/pubs, etc.) Check these and then focus on the historical details and ask the students to pick out from the text all the expressions that talk about the past, for example: *for over a thousand years, since Roman times, medieval, 17th-century, from the Stone Age, from ... to ..., in ..., dating from ...* Check understanding.
Divide the class up into small groups of two to four students and allocate to each group one of the places of interest in your own town/area. Give them about 5 minutes to write a few sentences about it, circulating to help and encourage. Anyone who finishes early should be encouraged to write a few general sentences that could be used for an introduction. The class finally present a *Where to go and what to see in ...*, with the various groups reading out their contributions.

Practice 2 *(15 minutes)*

If your town is twinned with another town in a different country, use this fact as an introduction to the idea of a group of English-speaking tourists coming to visit. (Otherwise talk about an exchange programme.) Explain that the class are now going to try their hands at being travel agents. A group of fifteen English-speakers of all ages are coming to their town for a day's visit and the class have been asked to organize their programme, from 9am until 9pm, including all meals and refreshments. Divide the class into groups and give them about 5 minutes to write their timetables.

Conclusion *(5 minutes)*

Listen to the different timetable suggestions and vote on the best one, making sure that time has been allowed for food, drink, rest, taking photos and buying souvenirs.

Homework

Students could write a more extended description of a place of interest and illustrate it with either a photograph or a drawing. This work could then be combined into a wall display about the local area and its various attractions. They might also like to find out about places in Britain they would be interested in visiting.

15 Where to go and what to see

Rochester Upon Medway
Heritage, History and Hospitality

Castle

Guildhall

Positioned midway between London and the Channel ports, the city of Rochester has stood guard over the river Medway crossing for over a thousand years. Kings and queens, soldiers and sailors, pilgrims and traders have all passed through Rochester. There has been a settlement here since Roman times and part of the medieval city walls can still be seen today in the High Street.

Closer to our own times, there are strong associations with the famous author Charles Dickens who lived near Rochester and set many of his novels in this region. Every year there is a Dickens Festival in May/June, when over 10,000 people dress up in costume and provide street entertainment.

Today Rochester is easily accessible from London by rail and road and is a handy stopping off point for visitors coming from the Channel ports. There are many craft and antique shops, as well as tea rooms, coffee shops and old pubs. The city is a master in the art of hospitality – it has been welcoming visitors for centuries ■

Cathedral

DON'T MISS...

The Charles Dickens Centre
Dramatic audiovisual displays bring the world of Dickens to life.

Guildhall Museum
17th-century building containing exhibits on local history from the Stone Age to the present day.

Motor Cycle Museum
Collection of British motorcycles from 1921 to 1977.

Restoration House
Where Charles II stayed in 1660 on his way to London to be crowned king.

Rochester Castle
A particularly fine example with gardens and good views up the river.

Rochester Cathedral
An impressive church dating from 1080.

Dickens Festival

Teacher's notes

16 In the news this week ...

Aim	To work on short news items – writing and answering questions about facts and figures and writing headlines.
Preparation	Copy and cut up the handout on page 61 – one copy per six students, so each student can have one news item.
(Optional)	Bring in a copy of an English newspaper.

Introduction *(5 minutes)*

Introduce the idea of news, either by showing an English newspaper and pointing out one or two of the main articles, or by asking students to tell you briefly about some of the main news items of that day/week. Talk about how headlines are used to attract our attention and make us want to read the article but are not always very informative.

Presentation *(10 minutes)*

Write the six headlines from the news items on the board. Divide the class into three groups. Each group works on two of the headlines and tries to imagine what the articles would be about. Students should work individually and write one sentence for each headline. Have a whole class feedback asking students to read their sentences and note how many different ideas there are. (You may like to keep these on the board to compare with the real articles later.)

Practice *(30 minutes)*

Divide the class into six groups and give each member of the group the same news item. They should read this carefully, making sure they understand it fully by asking you about any vocabulary or using a dictionary. They should also check pronunciation. Within the groups, students work in pairs to write out five questions on a piece of paper, leaving space for the answers. Stress that the questions need to be clear and correct as another group will be answering them. They should put the headline on the top of the paper as a title.
When everyone is ready, each pair finds another pair who has worked on a different article. First they exchange questions and read these, asking one another for clarification if necessary. Then they take it in turns to read out their article to the other pair, who listen carefully and attempt to note down the answers to the questions. When both pairs have answered the questions, they re-exchange papers and the answers are marked and corrected by the question-setters.
A whole class feedback can identify and congratulate those who managed to answer all five questions correctly and can compare the actual articles with those that were imagined in the first presentation phase. Was anybody close to the real thing?
(Note: if time and interest allow, it is possible for each pair to work with a third pair, reading their item again and answering questions on another article. In this case, each member of the pair needs to write out a separate set of questions.)

Conclusion *(5 minutes)*

Read out the following short item and invite everyone to write a headline – the more eye-catching and intriguing, the better.
Here's the latest thing for shoppers in large supermarkets – a mini tram-train! It allows customers to sit in comfy seats and just put out their hands to choose what they want. And you don't need a ticket!

Homework

To write a short news item, complete with headline, on some small local event that has happened that week.

16 In the news this week ...

British drivers

BRITISH DRIVERS are the safest and most polite in Europe, according to a survey by Uniroyal, the tyre manufacturer. The survey said that just one in ten London drivers do not stop at red lights and that nine in ten obeyed parking laws. Mobile phones, however, may prove to be a problem as some drivers using phones have smashed into the car in front of them.

CENTRAL HEATING IN CAVES

A scientist is trying to help some of Britain's endangered bats to survive by providing central heating in a cave. The rare bat, which has a wingspan of up to 45cm, now only numbers about 5,000. Two special heaters in the cave will give the bats almost perfect conditions.

NUMBERS CHANGE AGAIN

Telephone numbers in six areas of the United Kingdom will have to be changed because of the increasing number of telephone connections. In April these areas will be given new area codes, all starting with 02. In London the 0171 and 0181 codes will be combined into an 020 code covering the whole of the capital.

A rich kid

A 14-YEAR-OLD BOY has become Britain's youngest millionaire and has made his money by selling top motorcars to customers all over the world. His amazing success means that he owns a mobile phone, wears designer clothes and has his own chauffeur who drives him around.

First women in charge

The Royal Navy has changed its 400-year-old rules and appointed two women to be in charge of warships and 17 crew members. Both women are in their late twenties and have considerable experience. There are now about 700 women at sea altogether and discussions are taking place as to whether they are to be allowed to serve on board submarines.

A VALUABLE BUTTERFLY

A tiny brooch that was bought at a junk shop for only 50p was sold yesterday in London for £13,225. The brooch is shaped like a butterfly and is over a hundred years old. The owner thought the stones were of no value but in fact they were diamonds.

Teacher's notes

17 Lots of letters

Aim	To study and practise different styles of letter writing for different occasions.
Preparation	Copy the handout on page 63 – one copy per student. Bring in several pairs of scissors for students to cut up the individual cards.

Introduction *(5–10 minutes)*

Introduce the topic by saying that you had to write eight different letters last weekend. Invite the class to guess what different occasions could have prompted them, for example:
*an invitation
a request for information
a thank you letter
a good luck letter
a letter making a booking
a get well soon letter,* etc.
Try to list as many different types of letters as you can. Which are the most difficult to write?

Presentation *(10 minutes)*

Give out the handouts and look at the six types of letter described in the boxes and the six extracts. Students work individually and then in pairs to match the extract with the type of letter it comes from. Draw attention to the useful expressions, namely:
*I/we would be delighted if ...
I should like to ...
It is with regret that ...
I am pleased to ...
hope ...
let me know ...
to inform you that ...*

Practice 1 *(15 minutes)*

Write six more types of letter on the board:
*apologies
complaints
thank you
congratulations
good luck
get well soon*
Divide the class into groups of three to five students. Each group now works on writing a suitable sentence for each of these occasions. For example:
*I am sorry you have been disturbed by my television.
Please investigate the matter and let me know what action you intend to take.*

*Thank you for the new scarf, which will be most useful this winter and was a very generous present.
I was so glad to hear of your new position and send my warmest congratulations.
I thought I would write to wish you all the best in your exams.
I'm sorry to hear that you are not feeling so well and do hope that you will be better soon.*
When they are ready, give out scissors. They cut up the blank boxes and write the sentences in six of them and the occasions in a further six.

Practice 2 *(10 minutes)*

Collect these in and then redistribute them so that each group has a set of twelve cards written by another group. These are placed on the desk in front of them face down. Students now take it in turns to turn over two cards to see if they match (i.e. the extract suits the occasion). If not, they turn them face down again. If they do match, they keep the pair. The student with the most pairs wins.
Note: if time allows, this can be extended by cutting out the first six cards as well and adding these to the set. Sets can also be passed round and compared.

Conclusion *(5–10 minutes)*

People write fewer letters nowadays because we have other means of communication such as the phone, e-mail, etc. Are there some occasions when only a letter is suitable and why?

Homework

Students can choose one or two of the extracts and occasions and expand these into full letters.

Key
job acceptance: I am pleased to accept your offer ... change of address: We shall be moving ... bookings: I should like to reserve ... resignation: It is with regret that ... bon voyage: Have a wonderful stay ... invitations: We would be delighted if you could join us ...

17 Lots of letters

job acceptance	bookings	bon voyage
change of address	resignation	invitations
We would be delighted if you could join us to celebrate our wedding at 10.30am at St James Church, Crawley.	I should like to reserve a table for 10 for 12.30 on Wednesday 18 October.	I am pleased to accept your offer of the post of Personal Assistant, starting on September 1st.
Have a wonderful stay and do let me know what life is like over there.	We shall be moving on June 1st and hope you will visit us once we are settled in.	It is with regret that I have to inform you of my intention to leave the company.

From *Instant Lessons 2 Intermediate* edited by Peter Watcyn-Jones © PENGUIN Books 2000

Teacher's notes

18 Telling stories

Aim	To develop storytelling and editing skills.
Preparation	Copy the handout on page 65 – one copy per student.

Introduction (5 minutes)

Write on the board the following question:
What makes a good story?
Invite answers and list them, for example: *an interesting story or characters, suspense, a good beginning and end,* etc.

Presentation (10 minutes)

Give out the handouts and read the story with the class. Explain that they are going to transform this boring account into an exciting short story about modern times. First they are going to expand the bare bones with details and descriptive words. Do the first sentence together as an example and list on the board some of the different ways it could be expanded to paint a much more vivid picture. For example:
Feeling very tired, Tom came home to his small untidy flat after a long day's work in the factory.
OR *It was a cold November evening and Tom was 34 years old when he came home after two months of looking for work and decided things had to change.*
OR *Feeling very pleased with himself, Tom came home after a few drinks in the pub to celebrate his promotion and salary increase at work.*
Invite other suggestions, noting how the first sentence will set the tone for much of what follows.

Practice 1 (10 minutes)

Students work individually to expand the story, adding details and descriptions to the basic story outline. Circulate to give encouragement and ideas but do not correct work.

Practice 2 (10 minutes)

The students now work as editors. Take in the stories and redistribute them so that each person has a story written by someone else. Their job is to correct this story, using a different coloured pen, to make it accurate and well written. Encourage them to check spelling and grammar and put in any improvements they can think of. Lastly they think of a possible beginning and ending and note these in the box.

Practice 3 (10 minutes)

The story now goes to a third student who copies out the story correctly, incorporating the beginning and the ending suggested and making the whole thing sound as good as possible.

Conclusion (10 minutes)

Once the final drafts are ready, students can form groups and read one another's. Some examples can be read to the class and a few chosen for special congratulations. Invite comments on the writing and editing phases.

Homework

Students choose one of the versions they particularly liked and write this out in detail to make an interesting story.

18 Telling stories

Tom came home after work. His wife came back late. They had dinner and watched television. That night they could not sleep because of loud noises. Next morning they decided to move.

Expansion

Beginning and ending

Teacher's notes

19 Create a word puzzle

Aim	To create a simple word puzzle, writing clues and choosing the vocabulary.
Preparation	Copy the handout on page 67 – one copy per student and an extra copy per 4–6 students.

Introduction *(5 minutes)*

Conduct a quick class survey to find out how many students like or do crosswords and word puzzles. What sort? Why do they like them? Also find out why the not-so-keen don't like them!

Preparation *(10 minutes)*

Give out the handouts and look at the completed word puzzle on the subject of sport. Draw attention to the hidden vertical word *athletics* and to the way the word puzzle is constructed. Ask the class to suggest clues for each answer. For example, for *racket: You need one to play tennis*; for *helmet: You wear it to protect your head*, etc. Write clues on the board as models and show how you can read the hidden word downwards once you have solved all the clues, using the number of letters to help you.

Practice *(25 minutes)*

Divide the class into groups of between four and six students who are going to work together to create a word puzzle. Give each group a theme from which they must choose their vocabulary and a hidden word of nine letters (to be kept a closely guarded secret), which will form the backbone of their word puzzle. Here are some suggestions:

theme	hidden word
music	*orchestra*
travelling	*passenger*
entertainment	*rehearsal*
household possessions	*furniture*
the human body	*eyelashes*
food and drink	*vegetable*

First they write their hidden word downwards and then they find other words from their particular topic area to make up this word. They work on clues to enable others to find the words and thus discover the secret word. When each group is ready, give them a new clean handout to write out the clues, leaving the word puzzle grid blank but putting in the correct number of squares to indicate the number of letters. They should also write the theme and their own names.

Conclusion *(10 minutes)*

Collect in the sheets and redistribute so that each group now has a word puzzle to complete. See if all groups can do this and find the hidden word. Ask for feedback on how good the clues were and how well chosen the vocabulary was.

Homework

To make up a word puzzle with clues, either on a subject of their choice or on a topic area that you would like to revise.

19 Create a word puzzle

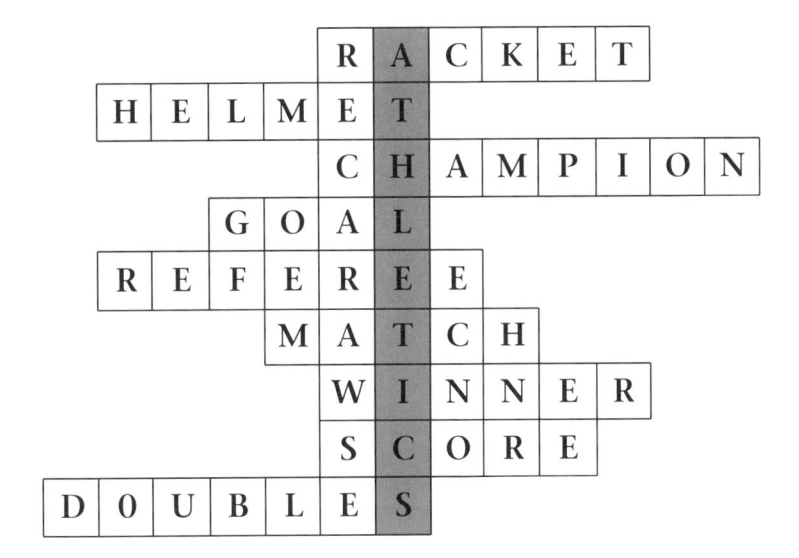

```
      R A C K E T
H E L M E T
      C H A M P I O N
    G O A L
R E F E R E E
    M A T C H
    W I N N E R
    S C O R E
D O U B L E S
```

1 _____

2 _____

3 _____

4 _____

5 _____

6 _____

7 _____

8 _____

9 _____

Teacher's notes

20 Looking after yourself

Aim	To be able to write simple warnings and advice – *do*s and *don't*s.
Preparation	Copy the handout on page 69 – one copy per student.
(Optional)	Bring in large pieces of paper for the students to use to present their leaflets.

Introduction *(5 minutes)*

Talk about some plans you have for going to the beach. Ask the students if they go, what activities they like to do there and what dangers there could be. Note some of these on the board.

Presentation *(10 minutes)*

Give out the handout and look at it together, explaining any vocabulary and pointing out the use of the imperative. Focus attention on the *do*s and *don't*s and explain that one *do* and one *don't* is missing each time and has been written at the bottom of the sheet.
Students work individually to put the instructions in the correct places. Check all answers.

Practice *(30 minutes)*

Tell the students that they are now going to work together in small groups to write a similar advice leaflet on this subject:
Keeping yourself fit and healthy

Ask them to suggest various aspects, for example: *diet, exercise, fresh air, sleep, stress, alcohol, tobacco*, etc. Write these on the board. The students now work together in pairs/groups to think of some *do*s and *don't*s for each aspect. Those students who work faster could try to write several under each heading. They could also think about illustrations. Circulate to give help and encouragement.
The final leaflets could be presented to the class in several ways: either written on a large sheet of paper and held up for all to see, or read out so that you can note the different *do*s and *don't*s on the board, or written out on the back of the handout and passed from group to group.

Conclusion *(5 minutes)*

What do members of the class do to keep fit? Is there anyone who does all the *do*s and none of the *don't*s?!

Homework

To write this out as a finished leaflet with some illustrations/design.

Key

Swimming: Do swim in company. Don't swim for at least an hour after meals.
If you get into difficulty: Do remain calm. Don't exhaust yourself.
Diving: Do check the depth of the water first. Don't dive into shallow water.
Windsurfing: Do keep out of the way of swimmers. Don't sail at night.
Fishing from rocks: Do wear highly visible clothing. Don't fish alone.

20 Looking after yourself

A GUIDE TO BEACH SAFETY

Swimming
✓ DO:
read warning notices first
✗ DON'T:
swim if you feel unwell
_____
_____

Diving
✓ DO:
think before you dive
✗ DON'T:
forget to look for hidden obstacles
_____
_____

Fishing from rocks
✓ DO:
be careful of extra large waves
✗ DON'T:
forget to wear shoes that do not slip
_____
_____

If you get into difficulty
✓ DO:
float on your back
✗ DON'T:
panic
_____
_____

Windsurfing
✓ DO:
check your equipment
✗ DON'T:
sail unless you are a good swimmer
_____
_____

sail at night
fish alone
check the depth of the water first
exhaust yourself
keep out of the way of swimmers

swim for at least an hour after meals
remain calm
swim in company
dive into shallow water
wear highly visible clothing

Grammar: Lessons 21–30

21 Past Simple v Present Perfect

Aim	To contrast the use of the Past Simple and Present Perfect.
Preparation	Copy the handout on page 71 – one copy per student. Also complete, copy and cut out the cards on page 73 – one set per 10 students.

Introduction (5 minutes)

Introduce the topic by telling students about something you enjoy doing. For example:
I enjoy visiting my friends in Newcastle.
Now tell the students how often you've been there and when was the last time.
I've been several times this year.
I last went to see them two weeks ago.
Now ask a student:
What about you? What do you enjoy doing?
When the student has answered, ask him/her how often s/he has done it in the past year/month and when s/he last did it. In pairs, the students now ask each other. Finally, ask a few students to tell you what they have found out about their partner.

Presentation (15 minutes)

Explain that you are looking at the difference in the use of the Past Simple and the Present Perfect. Take an example from one of the students:
X likes doing Y. When did s/he last do this?
Before giving the answer, draw a time line on the board:

```
                    ×
─────────────────────────────────▶
past              last         present
                  week
```

Point out to the students that we know WHEN the action took place. Because of this we use the Past Simple.
Now ask: *How often has s/he done this?* As the students answer, draw another time line on the board:

```
─────────────────────────────────▶
past                          present
```

Point out that you can't put an exact point on the time line because the answer doesn't tell us exactly when the actions took place.
Now ask the students: *Has anyone else ever done this?* When some students answer *Yes*, point out that again you don't know exactly when and, therefore, you use the Present Perfect.

Practice (20 minutes)

Activity A Students work either individually or in pairs. Check orally.
Now hand out a card (from page 73) to every student; it doesn't matter if there are some repeated cards. Then get them, one at a time, to ask another student:
Have you ever ... (been to Colombia)?
Yes.
When did you ... (go there)?
I (went there last year).

Conclusion (10 minutes)

Activity B Students do the activity in pairs. When they have discussed what changes have occurred, they should write down a list, showing what happened in the time of their grandparents and what has changed since then.

Homework

Activity C Make sure the students realize that some of the verbs here may be in the present tense.

(continued on page 72)

Key

A 1 got married   2 have bought   3 raged   4 have had   5 gave, moved   6 claimed   7 has never lost   8 wrote, has taken   9 has never paid   10 has always had

B When talking about the time of the grandparents, students use the Past Simple form. They use the Present Perfect form for what has happened since then.

C 1 bought   2 have not had   3 was not   4 tried   5 set off   6 live   7 turned   8 came   9 have often seen   10 have walked   11 did not realize   12 was   13 is/was   14 saw   15 shouted   16 was   17 rode   18 tried   19 rode   20 have avoided   21 have found   22 have not seen   23 am able/have been able   24 have been chased/am chased   25 never fall/have never fallen   26 have learned

Teacher's notes

21 Past Simple v Present Perfect

A Put the verbs in the correct form: Past Simple or Present Perfect.

1. Lee (get marry) .... in November 1999.
2. Mark and Daisy (buy) .... a house at the end of the street.
3. Storms (rage) .... over the southern half of the country in the winter of 2000.
4. We (have) .... a very good summer so far this year.
5. Ivy (give) .... the old photographs to the History Society when she (move) .... from the town.
6. The President (claim) .... victory before all the votes were counted.
7. The Chancellor (never lose) .... an election since 1995.
8. Darren (write) .... his first novel in ten days, but he (take) .... two years to write the second and it is still not finished.
9. Brent (never pay) .... for a meal since he left college.
10. He (always have) .... very generous friends, although he's a very difficult person.

B Discuss with a partner and look at ways life has changed for your families in the last fifty years. Compare what your grandparents did with what you can do. Make a list. This should be in sentence form, for example:

My grandfather and grandmother had their holidays at home. We have always gone abroad for our holidays.

C Put the verbs into the correct form: Present Simple, Past Simple or Present Perfect.

Last week, I (1 buy) .... a bike. I (2 not have) .... a bike for thirty years, so I (3 not be) .... confident when I (4 try) .... to ride it. I (5 set off) .... on the first morning down the street where I (6 live) .... and then (7 turn) .... to ride along the canal. Since I (8 come) .... to live here, I (9 often see) .... people riding along the canal when I (10 walk) .... there, but I (11 not realize) .... how bad the path (12 be) .... for cyclists. It (13 be) .... very narrow. When I (14 see) .... a walker, I (15 shout), but on one occasion, it (16 be) .... too late and I (17 ride) .... into the walker. But the worst time was when I (18 try) .... to avoid a dog and (19 ride) .... straight into the canal.

Since then I (20 avoid) .... the canal. I (21 find) .... a very nice, quiet road. I (22 not see) .... any walkers there and I (23 be able) .... to ride more confidently. Sometimes, I (24 be chased) .... by a dog or a fox, but I (25 never fall) .... off the bike. One day I will go back to the canal – when I (26 learn) .... to control the bike properly.

Teacher's notes

Activity A Hand out a card to every student; it doesn't matter if there are some repeated cards. Then get them, one at a time, to ask another student:
Have you ever … (been to Colombia)?
Yes.
When did you … (go there)?
I (went there last year).

21 Past Simple v Present Perfect (continued)

Prepare some cards giving the names of places your students will know. These should not be famous international places as it is unlikely that many of your students will have visited them. It is better to choose places in the town, city or country where you live.

Have you ever been to ....? Yes. When did you go there?	Have you ever been to ....? Yes. When did you go there? ....
Have you ever been to ....? Yes. When did you go there?	Have you ever been to ....? Yes. When did you go there? ....
Have you ever been to ....? Yes. When did you go there?	Have you ever been to ....? Yes. When did you go there? ....
Have you ever been to ....? Yes. When did you go there?	Have you ever been to ....? Yes. When did you go there? ....
Have you ever been to ....? Yes. When did you go there?	Have you ever been to ....? Yes. When did you go there? ....

From *Instant Lessons 2 Intermediate* edited by Peter Watcyn-Jones © Penguin Books 2000

Teacher's notes

22 Conditional 1

Aim	To show the form and use of the first conditional.
Preparation	Copy and cut out the cards and dominoes on page 75 – one set per pair. Copy the handout on page 77 – one copy per student.

Introduction *(5 minutes)*

Start by talking about what you like to do: *go fishing, go to the theatre, play football, watch TV, read biographies*, etc. Then continue:
If I finish early this evening, I'll go to see (whatever film is on at the local cinema); and if it's fine at the weekend, I'll play football/go walking/work in the garden, etc.
Write the sentence on the board. Then ask some students:
What will you do if you get home early tonight/tomorrow?
What will you do if the weather's fine at the weekend?
Accept part answers such as: *I'll see my friend. I'll play tennis.*
Write the questions on the board. Students ask similar questions in pairs.

Presentation *(15 minutes)*

Point out to the students the form of the sentences.
IF + Present Simple // modal (usually WILL or WON'T) + main verb without TO
Explain to the students that when we use this form of the conditional, we are talking about something that is not unlikely to happen, although we can't be certain that it will happen. For example: *If the weather's fine at the weekend, I'll go fishing.* You can't be certain that you'll go fishing. But this is what you'll do in particular, not unlikely circumstances. Point out that *won't* is the contraction of *will not*.
Now give some more examples and write them on the board:

If I win some money, I'll have a holiday in India.
If it rains on Sunday, I won't play football.
If my cousin visits me, I'll take him to see (whatever is interesting locally).
If I wake up early tomorrow, I'll go surfing.
Ask students which the *if* clauses are. Underline the verbs in the *if* clauses, making it clear that they are in the Present Simple form.

Practice *(20 minutes)*

Activity A Play the game in pairs. Give each pair a set of dominoes and explain that they have to match the second part of one domino to the first part of another to make a full sentence. They should arrange the dominoes to make a square. Put this shape guide on the board to help them:

Activity B Put the students into groups. Give each group a set of the cards. In turn each student takes a card and has to complete the sentence, either with the *if* clause or the main clause.

(continued on page 76)

Key

A If it rains on Sunday /// I won't have to water the plants.
If I can't have a party at my parents' house /// I'll go and live with my friends.
If I don't study tonight /// I'll fail the exam tomorrow.
If our local football team play Manchester United /// they won't win the match.
If Josie doesn't want to come /// we'll go without her.

If I get married /// I'll wear a white dress.
If that new play is on /// Peter will probably get tickets.
If Tom and Andy don't arrive soon /// they won't catch the train.
If Hannah makes any more mistakes /// she'll lose her job.
If Rachel doesn't go to the cinema with Liam /// he'll ask Saskia instead.

(continued on page 76)

22 Conditional 1

A

he'll ask Saskia instead	if it rains on Sunday	I'll go and live with my friends	if I don't study tonight
I'll wear a white dress	if that new play is on	I'll fail the exam tomorrow	if our local football team plays Manchester United
they won't catch the train	if Hannah makes any more mistakes	Peter will probably get tickets	if Tom and Andy don't arrive soon
they won't win the match	if Josie doesn't want to come	we'll go without her	if I get married
I won't have to water the plants	if I can't have a party at my parents' house	she'll lose her job	if Rachel doesn't go to the cinema with Liam

B

If I see Katie, ………………………………	If the train's late, ………………………………
If my aunt comes next Wednesday, ……………	If I win £1 million, ………………………………
If it doesn't snow next winter, …………………	If you hear a noise in the night, …………………
If I have a baby, ………………………………	If my friend doesn't like the new car, …………………
If you don't work hard, ………………………………	If you don't get home early, ………………………………

Teacher's notes

Activity C Students have to match the two parts of the sentence. They can do this individually or in pairs. Give a time limit of five minutes, so that you can check the answers. Explain that the London Eye is the big wheel put up in London for the Millennium.

Conclusion *(10 minutes)*

Play the Consequence Game in groups of three to five students. You give the first statement: *If I meet Lucy tonight, I'll invite her to my party.* The groups write this at the top of a piece of paper. Each student in turn adds a sentence. They must begin by turning the main clause of the previous sentence into the *if* clause of the next sentence. Thus the first student must begin: *If I invite Lucy to my party, ...*
In this way the group gradually builds up a story. At the end, listen to all the stories.

Homework

Activity D Students complete the sentences.

Key

C 1 f   2 c   3 g   4 i   5 a   6 k   7 e   8 b   9 j   10 d   11 h

22 Conditional 1 (continued)

C Match the two parts of the sentences.

1 Mark will miss the train   a if they haven't got a map.
2 Their garden won't be beautiful   b if they bite you.
3 You'll have a good holiday   c if they don't look after it.
4 Monica will earn a lot of money   d if he asks her to.
5 They won't know the way   e if I go to London.
6 The business will lose money   f if he doesn't hurry.
7 I'll go on the London Eye   g if you go to the Mediterranean.
8 Some snakes will kill you   h if Rob eats her pizza.
9 There'll be an accident   i if she gets that job.
10 Patricia will marry Ray   j if they don't improve that road.
11 Annie will be angry   k if we don't modernize.

D Complete the sentences. Where there is the *if* clause, add a main clause; where there is a main clause, add an *if* clause.

1 We'll meet you on Friday ....
2 If the tiger escapes from the zoo, ...
3 If you catch a large fish, ...
4 There'll be a big reward ....
5 The river will flood ....
6 If I can't find the money, ...
7 The people will be very angry ....
8 If the company goes bankrupt, ...
9 If she goes to the party with Charlie, ...
10 The club will close ....

Find these words in the dictionary and translate them.
business, marry, the Mediterranean, improve, escape, reward, flood, go bankrupt

Teacher's notes

23 The article

Aim	To examine rules for the use of the definite article.
Preparation	Copy the handout on pages 79 and 81 – one copy per student.

Introduction (5 minutes)

Give the students the first handout. Ask them to read through the sentences at the top of the page, and in small groups set down the rules they know for the use of the definite and indefinite articles. They will probably mention the following: we use the indefinite article (*a/an*) when a person or thing is mentioned for the first time and is unknown, and we use the definite article (*the*) when we know the person or thing referred to.

Presentation (15 minutes)

Explain that you are now going to talk about the use of *the* and *a/an* and when we use no article. Prepare the table below on the board.

ARTICLE	EXAMPLE	RULE

Then write into the table the first and second columns as follows, eliciting from the students the rules to put into the third column.

ARTICLE	EXAMPLE	RULE
the	the woman at no. 8	when you know the person or thing you mean
	I met a boy. The boy was crying.	when you have talked about the person or thing before
	the President, the moon	when the person or thing is unique
	the United States of America	for countries that are a lot of states
	the Rhine, the Pyrenees	for rivers and ranges of mountains
a/an	I met a boy.	
	Did you buy a book at the sale?	
	Can you give me an orange?	when you don't know which boy, book or orange
(-)	I met boys from the village.	some boys, we don't how many – certainly not all the boys in the village
	A glass of water, please.	
	I like bread with my meals.	water and bread are used generally
	He lives in Spain.	for countries – but see exceptions above
	I want to climb Mt Everest.	for mountains – but not a mountain range

Practice (20 minutes)

Activity A The students work in groups. Check orally.

Activity B Again in groups, they must decide on the use made of the article. Check orally.

(*continued on page 80*)

Key	
A 1 an 2 the 3 a, the, The 4 a, the, The 5 a, the, a 6 an, the, The 7 the, a 8 a 9 a, The 10 a, the	B 1 c 2 a, e 3 c, c 4 b, e 5 e 6 a 7 c 8 a, c 9 c, a, c 10 d, e

(*continued on page 80*)

23 The article

> The sea around the coast of Newfoundland is very dangerous.
> A man broke into the home of the chief minister. The man stole the minister's seal of office.
> You won't eat a better pizza anywhere.
> There is an eclipse of the moon tonight.

A Underline the correct article.

1. He is very rich but he still drives (an/the) old car.
2. 'Where's Sue?'
   'She's in (a/the) bathroom.'
3. There's (a/the) lake in (a/the) park near my house. (A/The) lake is quite big.
4. We live in (a/the) big house in (a/the) west of Ireland. (A/The) house is over 200 years old.
5. 'Would you like (a/the) drink? There's orange juice in (a/the) fridge.'
   'Yes, please. Would you like (a/the) glass too?'
6. I'm reading (an/the) excellent book about (a/the) Second World War. (A/The) book was written by an American prisoner of war.
7. Does (a/the) town where you live have (a/the) cinema?
8. Have you got (a/the) cigarette? I've finished my packet.
9. She's got three children, (a/the) boy and two girls. (A/The) boy's name is Dan.
10. I'm going to (a/the) party tonight. It's at a club in (a/the) centre of town.

B Read the sentences and write a–e in the boxes, depending on how the articles underlined have been used.

a – when the person or thing is identified
b – when you have talked about the person or thing before
c – when the person or thing is unique
d – for countries that are a lot of states
e – for rivers or ranges of mountains

☐ 1 The Golden Gate Bridge is in San Francisco.
☐ 2 I visited the man who lives by the Thames.
☐ 3 The sun sets in the west.
☐ 4 He sent her an invitation to his party. The party will be on a boat on the Danube.
☐ 5 He is going to climb in the Andes on holiday.
☐ 6 The air in Berlin is very special.
☐ 7 Beijing is the capital of China.
☐ 8 The daughter of the king of Spain was married in Seville.
☐ 9 The Pope is the head of the Catholic Church.
☐ 10 Jimmy won some money last week. He's gone to the United States. He wants to go on a boat on the Mississippi.

Teacher's notes

Conclusion *(10 minutes)*

Activity C Students complete the letter by putting in the correct article.

Homework

Students write ten sentences describing the town where they live.

Key

C 1 an 2 / 3 a 4 the 5 the 6 / or the 7 / or the
8 The 9 the 10 a 11 the 12 / 13 the 14 the
15 the

23 The article (continued)

C Complete the letter by writing in the correct article (*the, a, an,* or / if no article is required).

Dear Bev,

I've just got back from three months in Berlin. It is (1)............ (2)............ exciting city. In recent years, it has changed a lot. There are (3)............ lot of new buildings in (4)............ centre of (5)............ city. I don't like (6)............ new buildings; but it is interesting. I've been to Berlin before and I visited (7)............ places I knew. These have changed. (8)............ old museums in the east of (9)............ city have been restored. There are now (10)............ lot of new cafés near (11)............ Gendarme Markt.

There are lots of (12)............ forests and parks and lakes in Berlin. You can escape from (13)............ city and feel you are in (14)............ country. And in (15)............ evening there is so much to do.

You'd love it there. Come with me next year!

All good wishes,

Jo

Teacher's notes

24 Conditional 2

Aim	To show the form and use of the second conditional.
Preparation	Copy the handouts on pages 83 and 85 – one copy per student. Cut up the cards in Activity B.

Introduction *(5 minutes)*

Ask a student: *What are you going to do on Saturday?* (Choose someone you expect will be doing some outside activity.) When you've found someone doing something out-of-doors, ask: *What would you do if it rained?* Then add to the question: *Rain is possible. Would you do something else?*
Then ask other students where they are going for their holiday. Respond to each one with a negative-feeling question. For example, if people say they are going skiing, ask them: *What would you do if there wasn't enough snow?* If people say they are going to a beach resort, ask them: *What would you do there if it rained?*
Write the questions on the board.

Presentation *(15 minutes)*

Remind students of the form of the earlier conditional and write on the board:
First Conditional
   IF + Present Simple // modal (usually WILL/WON'T) + main verb without TO
Give two examples:
If it rains on Sunday, I'll stay at home and watch TV.
If the school falls down, we'll move to a new building on the other side of the town.
Explain to the students that when we use this form of the conditional, we are talking about something that is quite likely to happen, but we can't be certain if it will happen or not.

Now write on the board:
Second Conditional
   IF + Past Simple // modal (usually WOULD/WOULDN'T) + main verb without TO
Give two examples:
If it rained on Sunday, I would stay at home and watch TV.
If the school fell down, we would move to a new building on the other side of the town.
Explain that we use this form when we are talking about something that is possible but unlikely (in the first example, you are in a country where it doesn't usually rain at this time of year). We often use the second conditional to talk about something which doesn't take place. It is more imaginary.
Elicit from students four or five questions beginning: *What would you do if ...?* Write the questions on the board and then get the students to question each other in pairs.

Practice *(20 minutes)*

Activity A Give students the handout. The students can work in pairs for the matching exercise. See which pair completes it first.

Activity B Put the students into groups. Give each group a set of the cards. In turn each student takes a card and has to complete the sentence, either with the *if* clause or the main clause.

(continued on page 84)

Key
A 1j 2e 3i 4c 5g 6b 7d 8a 9f 10h

(continued on page 84)

24 Conditional 2

A Work in pairs and see how quickly you can match the parts of the sentences.

1 If Mark came on Wednesday,
2 If you read a newspaper,
3 If that house was for sale,
4 If I had a pet elephant,
5 If the bank didn't extend their loan,
6 If it snowed now,
7 If Real Madrid lost another game,
8 If I were the teacher,
9 If a mamba snake bit you,
10 If you were on the moon,

a I wouldn't accept such poor work.
b we wouldn't be able to drive home.
c I would take it for walks in the park.
d they would be out of the World Cup.
e you'd know about the accident.
f you'd be dead in minutes.
g they'd have to sell the business.
h you'd be weightless.
i I'd buy it.
j we could go to the theatre together.

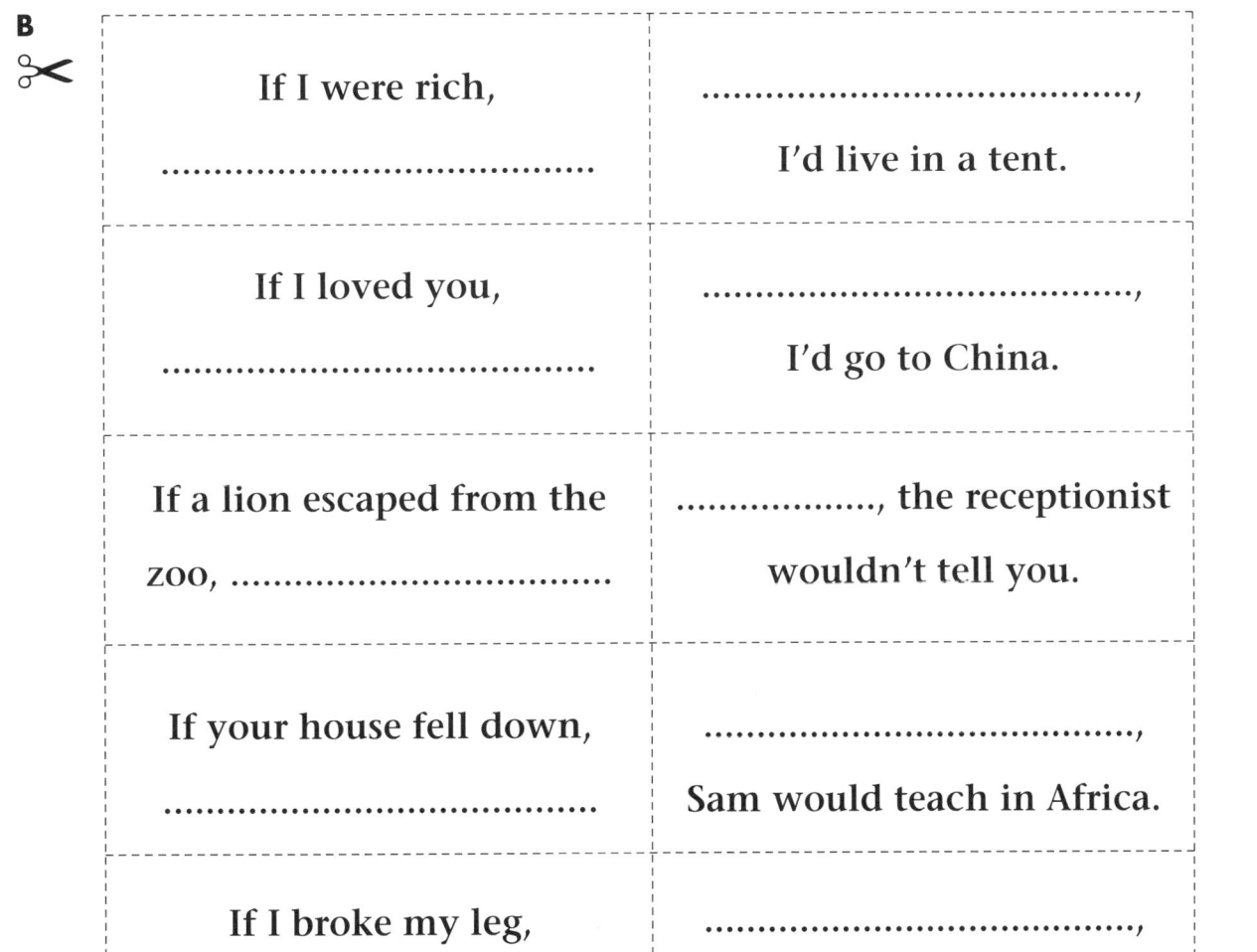

B

If I were rich, ...	................................, I'd live in a tent.
If I loved you, ...	................................, I'd go to China.
If a lion escaped from the zoo, ...	................................, the receptionist wouldn't tell you.
If your house fell down, ...	................................, Sam would teach in Africa.
If I broke my leg, ...	................................, Elisa would lose her job.

Teacher's notes

Conclusion *(10 minutes)*
Play the Consequence Game in groups of three to five students. You give the first statement:
If I met Lucy tonight, I'd invite her to my party.
The groups write this at the top of a piece of paper. Each student in the group adds a sentence. They must begin by turning the main clause of the previous sentence into the *if* clause of the next sentence. Thus the first student must begin:
If I invited Lucy to my party, ...
In this way the group gradually builds up a story. At the end, listen to all the stories.

Homework

Activity C This is a mixture of first and second conditionals. They complete the sentences by putting in the correct form of the verb and then decide on the use of the conditional form.

Key
C 1 give, a   2 would be able, b   3 were, b   4 will lose, a
   5 continues, a   6 would go back, b   7 got, b
   8 will be, a   9 would be able, b   10 will have to, a

24 Conditional 2 (continued)

C Complete the sentence, using the correct form of the verb in brackets. Then decide if it is:

a something that is quite likely to happen (Typ I)

b something that is unlikely to happen but is possible, or is more an imagined idea (Typ II)

Write *a* or *b* in the box at the beginning of each sentence.

= in der Lage sein

☐ 1 If I (give)............................ him the money, he'll be able to buy a new car.

☐ 2 If you went to Rome, you (be able)............................ to visit the Colosseum.

☐ 3 If you (be)............................ late, the boss would be angry.

☐ 4 If the boss is angry, you (lose)............................ your job.

☐ 5 If it (continue)............................ to rain, then the river will overflow.

☐ 6 If I liked the hotel, I (go back)............................ there.

☐ 7 If Maggy (get)............................ here on time, it would be a miracle.   *Wunder*

☐ 8 If you lose that ring, your grandmother (be)............................ very angry.

☐ 9 If you got up early tomorrow, we (be able)............................ to spend the whole day in the city.

☐ 10 If she doesn't like it, you (have to)............................ change your plans.

Teacher's notes

25 The passive

Aim	To show the form and use of the passive.
Preparation	Copy the handouts on pages 87 and 89 – one per student. Cut up the cards in Activity B.
(Optional)	Bring in objects made of different materials, e.g. wool, plastic, paper.

Introduction *(5 minutes)*

Get various items from students, for example a sweater, a plastic penholder, a cardboard cup – or bring them into the class yourself. Then hold up each one in turn and say:
This ... is made of ...
Write the sentences on the board. Then quickly ask several students:
What is this made of?
Practise the question. Then get the students to think of one object they have and ask the person next to them what it is made of.

Presentation *(15 minutes)*

Explain that you are talking about the passive. Show from the examples on the board that the passive form is made up of the verb *to be* and the past participle.
Now ask these two questions:
When did Columbus discover America?
When was America discovered?
Point out that the first question is about Columbus and therefore *Columbus* comes at the beginning of the answer:
Columbus discovered America in 1492.

The second question is about America, so *America* comes at the beginning of the answer. In order to do that we use the passive:
America was discovered in 1492.
Now think of a famous building in the district or region where you live and ask the students:
Who built it? When was it built?
Write the answers on the board:
X built the (famous building) in ...
The (famous building) was built in ...
Now give students the handout and draw their attention to text 1. Point out that we have used the passive in (i) and (ii) because we don't know who did the murder and who found the body. Verbs (iii) and (iv) are examples of the passive with modal verbs (modal + *be* + past participle). Now students look at texts 2 and 3. Ask them to explain the difference between them (answer: in text 2 we are focusing on what the police did, and in text 3 on who was arrested).

Practice *(20 minutes)*

Activity A Students work individually. Check orally.

Activity B Now put the students into small groups and give out the cards. They put all the cards face down on the desk. Each student in turn takes a card and has to reword the instruction in the passive. For example:
Don't lock this door. → This door mustn't be locked.

(continued on page 88)

Key

A   1 The work was finished at midnight.
2 *Hamlet* was written by Shakespeare.
3 The letter was posted by John this morning.
4 The tickets for the holiday will be booked soon.
5 Those trees were planted by the City Council in 1989.
6 A book about the Great Internet Disaster has not been written.
7 The lights were not switched off last night.
8 A fire was started near the school.
9 The lost diamond must be found.
10 The story of Mary's lucky escape cannot be told.

B   1 Coats mustn't be left here.
2 Dogs aren't allowed here.
3 All goods are checked by our staff.
4 Only qualified people are appointed.
5 All pupils must be taught two foreign languages at school.
6 This shop is cleaned every day.
7 The radio must be switched off after midnight.
8 A jacket and tie must be worn.
9 Every item on the agenda must be discussed.
10 The tickets must be collected half an hour before the performance.

(continued on page 88)

25 The passive

Text 1
Bigsy Malone, the well-known thief, <u>has been murdered</u> (i). His body <u>was found</u> (ii) in the canal last night. The people living in the area are very worried and say that the murderer <u>must be found</u> (iii). The police are reassuring them and insisting that the murderer <u>will be found</u> (iv).

Text 2
Last night, the police arrested Terence Mowbray. They found him at his girlfriend's flat in south London. They took him to the police station and charged him with the murder of Bigsy Malone. Last week, a fisherman found Bigsy's body in the canal.

Text 3
Last night, Terence Mowbray was arrested. He was found at his girlfriend's flat in south London. He was taken to the police station and was charged with the murder of Bigsy Malone. Last week, Bigsy's body was found in the canal.

A Rewrite these sentences using the passive form.

1. They finished the work at midnight.
2. Shakespeare wrote *Hamlet*.
3. John posted the letter this morning.
4. They will book the tickets for the holiday soon.
5. The City Council planted those trees in 1989.
6. Nobody has written a book about the Great Internet Disaster.
7. Nobody switched off the lights last night.
8. Someone started a fire near the school.
9. They must find the lost diamond.
10. Nobody can tell the story of Mary's lucky escape.

B

1 Don't leave coats here.	2 No dogs here. (use the verb *allow*)
3 Our staff checks all goods.	4 We only appoint qualified people.
5 Schools must teach all pupils two foreign languages.	6 We clean this shop every day.
7 Switch off the radio after midnight.	8 You must wear a jacket and tie.
9 We must discuss every item on the agenda.	10 You must collect the tickets half an hour before the performance.

Teacher's notes

Activity C Students work in pairs. Check orally.

Conclusion *(10 minutes)*

Activity D Students work individually. Check orally.

Homework

Activity E Students complete the dialogue.

Key

C These houses were built in 1895. The first four were built by the builder for his sons. For over thirty years, these houses were lived in only by members of his family. As more people came to live in the street, a primary school was built nearby. (The) children were sent to the school by their families. When the families grew up and the children left home, the houses were sold by the parents. The houses were changed inside by the new owners. Larger bathrooms were made. The wall between the lounge and the dining room was knocked down. The houses were made to look modern. Gradually, the character of the street has been changed.

D 1 The painting was stolen by thieves last night.
2 John (has) crashed his car again.
3 That job can be done by anyone.
4 All the tickets were sold yesterday morning.
5 All unsold tickets must be returned.
6 Richard (has) found these old coins in his garden.
7 This ancient pottery was found (has been found) on a farm.
8 The streetlights are switched on very late in summer.
9 My bicycle is kept in the cellar.
10 Make sure that the jar is sealed properly.

E 1 be read 2 is badly written 3 been praised 4 are paid 5 is written 6 been reviewed 7 be sold 8 was blamed 9 Is/Was the book written 10 is/was told

25 The passive (continued)

C Rewrite this paragraph using the passive form of the verbs underlined.

They <u>built</u> these houses in 1895. The builder <u>built</u> the first four for his sons. For over thirty years, only members of his family <u>lived</u> in these houses. As more people came to live in street, they <u>built</u> a primary school nearby. The families <u>sent</u> their children to the school. When the families grew up and the children left home, the parents <u>sold</u> their houses. The new owners <u>changed</u> the houses inside. They <u>made</u> larger bathrooms. They <u>knocked</u> down the wall between the lounge and the dining room. They <u>made</u> the houses look modern. Gradually, the street <u>has changed</u> its character.

D Write sentences with the underlined word as the focus. The sentences may be active or passive. Be careful! Choose the right tense!

1. Thieves / steal / <u>the painting</u> / last night.
2. <u>John</u> / crash / his car / again.
3. Anyone / can do / <u>that job</u>.
4. They / sell / <u>all the tickets</u> / yesterday morning.
5. You / must return / <u>all unsold tickets</u>.
6. <u>Richard</u> / find / these old coins / in his garden.
7. They / find / <u>this ancient pottery</u> / on a farm.
8. They / switch on / <u>the streetlights</u> / very late in summer.
9. I / keep / <u>my bicycle</u> / in the cellar.
10. Make sure that / you / seal / <u>the jar</u> properly.

E Complete the dialogue with the passive form of the verb.

Darren: This book will (1 read)......................... by millions of people.
Fiona: Really. It (2 badly write)......................... .
Darren: Badly!! It has (3 praise)......................... by the best critics.
Fiona: Some critics (4 pay)......................... to write good notices.
Darren: Rubbish! It is important that all criticism (5 write)......................... honestly.
Fiona: Has the book (6 review)......................... by the best critics?
Darren: Not in every case. But it will (7 sell)......................... because ordinary people will like it.
Fiona: I didn't. I thought it was boring. In the review I saw, the writer (8 blame)......................... for being dull and complicated.
Darren: I'm not dull and complicated!!
Fiona: (9 write the book)......................... by you?
Darren: Yes. In fact the story (10 tell)......................... by both of us. It's the story of our marriage!

Teacher's notes

26 Comparisons

Aim	To show the comparative and superlative forms for adjectives and how they are used.
Preparation	Copy and cut up the cards on page 91 – one set per group. Copy the handout on page 93 – one copy per student.

Introduction *(5 minutes)*

Get the three tallest students in the class to stand up. Then make a comparison, for example:
Lucia is tall, but Luis is taller. Luis is taller than Lucia. Dani is taller than Luis. Dani is the tallest.
Write this on the board. Then ask the students:
Who is taller, Greta or Joan?
Who is the shortest person in the class?
Who is the cleverest person in the class?
For the last question, make a joke of it and don't accept any of the answers. In the end, say: *It's me. I'm the teacher.*
Now get the students in pairs to ask each other similar questions.

Presentation *(15 minutes)*

Ask the students to guess what the topic of the lesson is – comparing things or people. Put three columns on the board.
POSITIVE COMPARATIVE SUPERLATIVE
Make the comparison with the tall students again and write *tall, taller, the tallest* in the appropriate columns. Then repeat with *short, shorter, the shortest*. Ask students for a rule. Note: always put *the* with the superlative form.
Now put three faces on the board:

Put a name under each face: Dave, Al and Luke. Then ask students to describe Dave. Elicit that he looks *happy*. Then ask them to compare Al and Dave and then ask about Luke. Write *happy, happier, the happiest* in the appropriate columns. Now ask about three mountains to elicit the forms *big, bigger, the biggest*, and write these in the appropriate columns.
Then ask about a famous city: *Is (Venice) a beautiful city?* Ask which city is more beautiful and finally which city they think is the most beautiful. Then write *beautiful, more beautiful, the most beautiful* in the appropriate columns. Now ask the students in groups to work out rules for the different forms. Finally point out two exceptions and write them on the board: *good, better, the best* and *bad, worse, the worst*.

Practice *(20 minutes)*

Activity A Put the students into groups and give each group a set of cards. The cards are placed face down on the table. Each student in turn takes a card and gives the forms not shown on the card. For example, if a student picks up *happy*, s/he must say *happier, the happiest*; if the student picks up *the oldest*, s/he must say *old, older*, etc.

(continued on page 92)

Key

A good, better, the best
happy, happier, the happiest
big, bigger, the biggest
small, smaller, the smallest
bad, worse, the worst
young, younger, the youngest
old, older, the oldest
important, more important, the most important

cheap, cheaper, the cheapest
dear, dearer, the dearest
pretty, prettier, the prettiest
beautiful, more beautiful, the most beautiful
large, larger, the largest
kind, kinder, the kindest
thin, thinner, the thinnest

(continued on page 92)

26 Comparisons

A

good	happier	big
the smallest	worse	young
older	important	cheaper
the dearest	the prettiest	more beautiful
larger	kind	thin

Teacher's notes

Activity B Students work in pairs on the text. Check orally.

Conclusion *(10 minutes)*

Activity C Students work individually. Check orally.

Homework

Students write ten sentences comparing their town or city with other places they know.

Key

B 1 most expensive 2 best 3 better 4 larger 5 worst
6 cheaper 7 cheapest 8 better 9 best

C 1 the largest 2 the hottest 3 higher 4 longer
5 colder 6 the biggest 7 the largest 8 the worst
9 more dangerous 10 the worst

26 Comparisons (continued)

B Look at the information about things to buy to help you clean the house. Then complete the text with the comparative or superlative form of one of these adjectives. You can use the adjectives more than once.

bad   cheap   expensive   good   large

C

PRODUCT	PRICE	SIZE	EFFECTIVENESS
Kleanrite	£5.90	500g	very good
Getklene	£2.40	250g	very poor
Briten	£7.60	1kg	poor
Bandirt	£4.30	250g	excellent
Dirtgone	£3.80	250g	good
WonderKlene	£6.00	500g	good

We looked at six products for cleaning the house. The (1).......................... per kilo was Bandirt. It cost £17.20 per kilo, but it was considered the (2).......................... . Dirtgone was also expensive. It was good, but Kleanrite was (3).......................... , especially for ovens. However, you had to buy Kleanrite in (4).......................... amounts than Bandirt. The (5).......................... product was Getklene. At £9.60 per kilo, it was (6).......................... than many of the other products. The (7).......................... was Briten. That was also considered poor, but it was (8).......................... than Getklene. Probably the (9).......................... product to buy is Kleanrite. It is very good and gives value for money.

Complete the sentences by writing the correct form of the adjectives in brackets.

1 Tokyo is (large).............................. city in Japan.
2 Phoenix is (hot).............................. place in the USA.
3 The Pyrenees are (high).............................. than the Urals.
4 The Amazon is (long).............................. than the Thames.
5 Milan is (cold).............................. than Naples in winter.
6 China has (big).............................. population in the world.
7 Russia has (large).............................. number of time zones of any country.
8 Mozambique has suffered (bad).............................. floods in its history.
9 The lion is (dangerous).............................. than the tiger.
10 Mexico City has (bad).............................. traffic problems in the whole of Central America.

Teacher's notes

27 Modals 1: *must, have to*

Aim	To explain how *must* and *have to* are used, both in form and function.
Preparation	Copy the handouts on pages 95 and 97 – one copy per student.

Introduction *(5 minutes)*

Draw a matchstick character on the board or show a picture of a man. Tell the class:
This is Will Johnson. He works in a shop. The shop opens at 9.00am, so he has to get there by 8.30am. He works in the clothing department so he has to wear smart clothes.
Now ask some of the students about Will Johnson. For example:
Christina, what time does Will Johnson have to get to work?
Ros, what sort of clothes does he have to wear?
Then continue:
Donna, what time do you have to be in school?
Then get the students to work in pairs to ask each other similar questions about themselves.

Presentation *(15 minutes)*

Tell the students you are going to talk about the difference between the use of *must* and *have to*. Put these sentences on the board:
You have to be at school by nine o'clock.
I must get up early tomorrow.
Point out that we use *have to* when there is an outside authority, for example for official regulations. We use *must* when it is the speaker's own authority:
You have to be at school by nine o'clock. (That is the rule of the school.)
You must be at school by nine o'clock today. (That is because I told you.)
We have to phone the office to say we'll be late. (That is the rule.)
We must phone the office to say we'll be late. (It's polite to do so.)
Ask the students to give you some examples for *must* and *have to* and write them on the board.

Then, using these examples, make the question form by asking various students. For example, if the sentences on the board are:
I must get a new car.
David has to work next Sunday.
ask the questions:
Jack, must you get a new car?
Rob, do you have to work next Sunday?
Only expect and encourage *Yes* or *No* answers to your questions. Then get the students to ask each other similar questions using the examples on the board, and to note when the answer is *No*.
Now point out the difference between *mustn't* and *don't have to*:
Jack mustn't get a new car. (It's forbidden.)
Rob doesn't have to work next Sunday. (It isn't necessary.)

Practice *(20 minutes)*

Activity A Get the students to match the three columns to make sentences. They then label them according to their function.

Activity B Students complete the sentences in pairs.

Activity C In pairs, students identify the rules according to their function.

(continued on page 96)

Key

A 1 My doctor told me I have to give up smoking. O
    2 It's a great book. You must read it. P
    3 In Britain you mustn't drive without wearing a seatbelt. F
    4 I want to pass this exam, so I must work much harder. P
    5 It's voluntary, so you don't have to do it. NN
    6 This bill has to be paid immediately. O

B 1 have to 2 must 3 don't have to 4 don't have to
   5 must 6 mustn't 7 must 8 mustn't 9 have to
   10 must
C Obligation from authority: 1, 2, 3, 6
   Forbidden: 7
   Not necessary: 4, 5

(continued on page 96)

27 Modals 1: *must, have to*

A The six sentences below are mixed up. Can you sort them out? Write them down then label them: O (obligation from an authority), P (personal duty), F (forbidden) or NN (not necessary).

1 My doctor told me I	don't have to	read it.
2 It's a great book. You	have to	be paid immediately.
3 In Britain you	must	do it.
4 I want to pass the exam, so I	has to	give up smoking.
5 It's voluntary, so you	mustn't	work much harder.
6 This bill	must	drive without wearing a seatbelt.

B Complete the sentences using *must, have to, mustn't* or *don't have to*.

1 To travel on the London Underground you _____ have a valid ticket.
2 I've put on weight again. I really _____ go on a diet.
3 Attendance at the meeting is optional, so you _____ come if you don't want to.
4 In Britain, you _____ pay a doctor if you are ill and he comes to see you. It's free.
5 'Have you seen the musical *Mama Mia*?'
   'No.'
   'Oh, it's brilliant! You _____ see it!'
6 It's a secret. So you _____ tell anybody!
7 You turned down a £60,000 a year job in Japan? You _____ be mad!
8 This is an exam, remember, so you _____ talk to anyone until it is over.
9 In Britain most children _____ wear a school uniform. (It's usually part of the school rules.)
10 The next time you visit Wales, you _____ come and stay with us.

C Here are some rules for a sports and social club. Decide which category each rule belongs to and write letters in the boxes: O (obligation from an authority), F (forbidden) or NN (not necessary).

1 All members have to pay their membership fee before the last day of the month.
2 Members have to wear suitable clothing for the event they are attending.
3 Members have to accompany their guests at all times.
4 Members do not have to register a guest in advance.
5 No member has to attend every general meeting.
6 New members have to be supported by two members if they wish to join the club.
7 Members must not give or lend their membership cards to non-members.

Teacher's notes

Conclusion *(10 minutes)*

Students work in groups to write their own rules for a club.

Homework

Activity D Students complete the sentences.

Key

D 1 mustn't   2 have to   3 mustn't   4 have to
   5 mustn't   6 don't have to   7 have to   8 don't have to

27 Modals 1: *must, have to* (continued)

D Look at the signs and complete the sentences using *have to*, *don't have to* or *mustn't*. Number 1 is an example.

1 You <u>mustn't</u> walk on the grass.

2 You _____ keep your dog on a lead.

3 You _____ take photographs.

4 You _____ be quiet in the library.

5 You _____ smoke in here.

6 You _____ buy anything.

7 You _____ send in your application form by July 23rd.

8 You _____ fasten your seatbelt.

Teacher's notes

28 Modals 2: *can, could, be able to*

Aim	To explain how *can*, *could* and *be able to* are used, both in form and function.
Preparation	Copy the handouts on pages 99 and 101 – one copy per student.

Introduction *(5 minutes)*

Ask the students some question using *can*. (They can be absurd.)
1 Can you run from ... to ... (Madrid to Toledo)?
2 Can you eat fifty eggs at one time?
3 Can I go to a party next Saturday?
4 Can you help me?
5 Can you travel from England to France by train?
6 Can you see the sea from your bedroom window?
Write the questions on the board, numbered 1–6, and the answers as they come. In pairs, students ask each other similar questions.

Presentation *(15 minutes)*

Explain that you are going to talk about the uses of *can*, *could* and *be able to*. Put the following table on the board:

	CAN	COULD	BE ABLE TO
1 Ability			
2 Possibility			
3 Request /Permission			

Remind the students of the questions you gave them in the introduction. Ask them to help you categorize them on the board. (Questions 1 and 2 are ability, 3 and 4 are requests/permissions, and 5 and 6 are possibilities.)
Now rewrite the ability questions with *be able to* in the third column: *Are you able to run ...?* etc.

Rewrite the possibility and request questions with *could* in the second column: *Could I go to a party next Saturday?* etc.
Point out that even though you can make a request using *could*, the answer is always with *can*:
Could I go to the cinema?
Yes, you can.
Now show that for the past, we can use *was able to* or *could*:
When I was young, I was able to run/I could run in the marathon. (But now I can't. I'm too old.)
But for the past with possibility, we use *could + have + past participle*:
I could have got that job if I was younger. (It was possible in the past, but it didn't happen.)
Finally, show that *can't* is often used like *mustn't*. Show the sign *No Parking*. Point out this can be rephrased:
You mustn't/can't park here.
Also point out that you cannot use another modal verb with *can* or *could*; but that this is possible with *be able to*:
If it's not too late, I would be able to meet him.
If you go now, you should be able to catch the bus.

Practice *(20 minutes)*

Activity A Students work individually. Check orally.

Activity B Students work in pairs. Check orally.

(continued on page 100)

Key

A 1 Were you able 2 can't 3 can 4 was able
   5 never be able 6 Can/Could 7 could 8 can't
   9 was able 10 can't

B 1 Last week, you/I/we couldn't park in this street.
   2 That bag is very small. You can take it on the plane as hand luggage.
   3 It's a very frightening film. Children under sixteen can't see it.
   4 I'm old enough. I should be able to go in.
   5 You can use all credit cards here.
   6 You can't smoke here.
   7 Non-residents can use the hotel restaurant.
   8 Can/Could I drive your car?
   9 There's no early train on Sunday. You can't get to London before 6 o'clock in the evening.
   10 If you finished that work tonight, you would be able to go away/you could go away for the weekend.

(continued on page 100)

28 Modals 2: *can, could, be able to*

A Complete the sentences with *can, can't, could, couldn't* or *be able to*. Make sure you use the correct tense.

1 ....(you) to visit your aunt when you were on holiday?
2 Is it true that cats ....(not) swim?
3 A camel .... live for eight days without water.
4 Frank .... to go round the world when he won the money on the lottery.
5 It's no use. I'll ....(never) to use a computer.
6 .... we keep a crocodile as a pet, please?
7 Fifty years ago, you .... buy a good meal at that restaurant for under £5.
8 Help that old lady across the road. She ....(not) see well.
9 He said he was ill. But he .... to go and watch his favourite football team.
10 No! You ....(not) go out tonight!

B Rewrite the sentences using *can, can't, could, couldn't* or *be able to*.

1 Last week, there was no parking in this street.
2 That bag is very small. They'll let you take it on the plane as hand luggage.
3 It's a very frightening film. No children under sixteen.
4 I'm old enough. They should let me go in.
5 All credit cards accepted here.
6 No smoking.
7 The hotel restaurant is open to non-residents.
8 Let me drive your car.
9 There's no early train on Sunday. It's impossible to get to London before 6 o'clock in the evening.
10 If you finished that work tonight, they would let you go away for the weekend.

Teacher's notes

Conclusion *(10 minutes)*
Activity C Students work in pairs or small groups.

Homework
Activity D The students complete the dialogue at home. If here is time in the next lesson, they can act it out.

Key

C 1 g 2 b 3 a 4 f 5 c 6 d 7 b 8 a 9 e 10 b

D 1 can/could   2 can't   3 can   4 can/could
   5 can't   6 Can't   7 be able   8 can't   9 could/can
   10 can   11 can

28 Modals 2: *can, could, be able to* (continued)

C How are *can* and *could* used in these sentences? Write a–g.

a = ability   b = possibility   c = past ability   d = past possibility
e = request or asking permission   f = giving and refusing permission
g = forbidden (not allowed)

☐ 1 Children under sixteen can't go in.
☐ 2 Can I use this mobile phone in Canada? Will it work?
☐ 3 I can't ride a bicycle.
☐ 4 All right. You can come with us to the athletics match.
☐ 5 When Joe was young, he could play the guitar like a rock'n'roll star.
☐ 6 Pat couldn't have written that essay. He doesn't know anything about the history of Brazil.
☐ 7 There are three roads you can take to get to the race course.
☐ 8 Can a hedgehog travel faster than a snail?
☐ 9 Can I see you tonight?
☐ 10 Can you travel by bus from Trafalgar Square to Piccadilly Circus?

D Complete the following dialogue with *can*, *could* or *be able*.

Sue: Martin, (1)................. you lend me £150?

Martin: Sorry, I (2).................(not). What do you want £150 for?

Sue: So I (3)................. buy those tin statuettes of musicians in the new shop. They'll look good in my room. I (4)................. pay you back next month.

Martin: Sorry! I (5).................(not). I'm broke. (6).................(not) you get the money from the bank?

Sue: I'm overdrawn already at the bank. If you won't lend me the money, I won't (7)................. to buy them. Then next week they'll be sold.

Martin: You (8).................(not) be sure of that.

Sue: They will be. I know.

Martin: All right. I suppose I (9)................. lend it to you. But (10)................. you definitely pay me back next month?

Sue: Oh yes, of course.

Martin: You didn't last time.

Sue: But I will this time. You (11)................. trust me.

From *Instant Lessons 2 Intermediate* edited by Peter Watcyn-Jones © Penguin Books 2000

Teacher's notes

29 Use of present tenses to express the future

Aim	To show how the Present Continuous and the Present Simple are used to express future events.
Preparation	Copy the handouts on pages 103 and 105 – one copy per student.

Introduction *(5 minutes)*

Tell students what your plans are. For example:
On Saturday, I'm painting my house. Next week, I'm visiting my parents. For the summer holidays, I'm flying to South Africa.
Then ask individual students:
What are you doing on Sunday/next week/in the holidays?
In pairs, students ask each other similar questions.

Presentation *(15 minutes)*

1 Explain that we often express the future by using one of the present forms. Write on the board:
PRESENT CONTINUOUS: *On Saturday, I'm painting the house.*
Tell them that by using the Present Continuous, you are making it clear that this plan is very definite. Contrast with:
I'm going to paint the house.
which is something you intend to do in a general way, but is not such a definite plan. Give other examples:
After the lesson, I'm seeing the head teacher.
The taxi's coming in five minutes.
Ask the students to give you some examples of their plans. Write a few on the board.

2 Now write on the board:
PRESENT SIMPLE: *Next week I'm flying to Madrid. The plane leaves at 10.50.*
Explain that we use the Present Simple when we are talking about official times and regular events. Then ask students:
When do the holidays start?
What time do you leave work tonight?
Get the students to give you some suggestions and write them on the board.

3 Remind students of the use of the Present Simple after *if*, for example:
If I see you next week, I'll give you that book.
Tell them that its use is similar after time conjunctions. Write on the board:
When I get to Cape Town, I'll visit some friends.
After I paint the house, I'll repair the car.
Before I paint the house, I'll buy some paint.
Tell them that with *while* you can also use the Present Continuous:
While I'm visiting friends in Cape Town, I'll tell them about your plans.

Practice *(20 minutes)*

Activity A Students should work in small groups or pairs to compose sentences from the information in the diary. The tense throughout should be the Present Continuous.

Activity B Working in pairs, the students decide on the use of the Present Simple in the sentences.

(continued on page 104)

Key

A On Monday at 1, I'm getting the train to Manchester, and at 7 I'm having dinner with the chairman. On Tuesday, from 9 to 12, I'm touring/having a tour of the factory. At 6, I'm playing golf with the chairman. On Wednesday morning, I'm returning to London. Between 1 and 2, I'm having lunch with my wife at Heathrow, then in the afternoon I'm flying to Madrid. In the evening, I'm having dinner with a Spanish customer. On Thursday morning, I'm flying back to London and in the evening I'm going to my son's 25th birthday party. On Friday morning, I'm doing the garden and in the afternoon I'm shopping with my wife. In the evening, we're going to the theatre. On Saturday morning, I'm playing tennis. In the afternoon, I'm doing the garden and in the evening I'm watching television.

B 1 a 2 b 3 a 4 b 5 c 6 c 7 c 8 c 9 c 10 b

(continued on page 104)

29 Use of present tenses to express the future

A Imagine you are Larry Keene, a senior manager with a textile company. This is your diary for next week. Write out your activities in full sentences. For example:

On Monday at 10, I'm meeting Frank West.

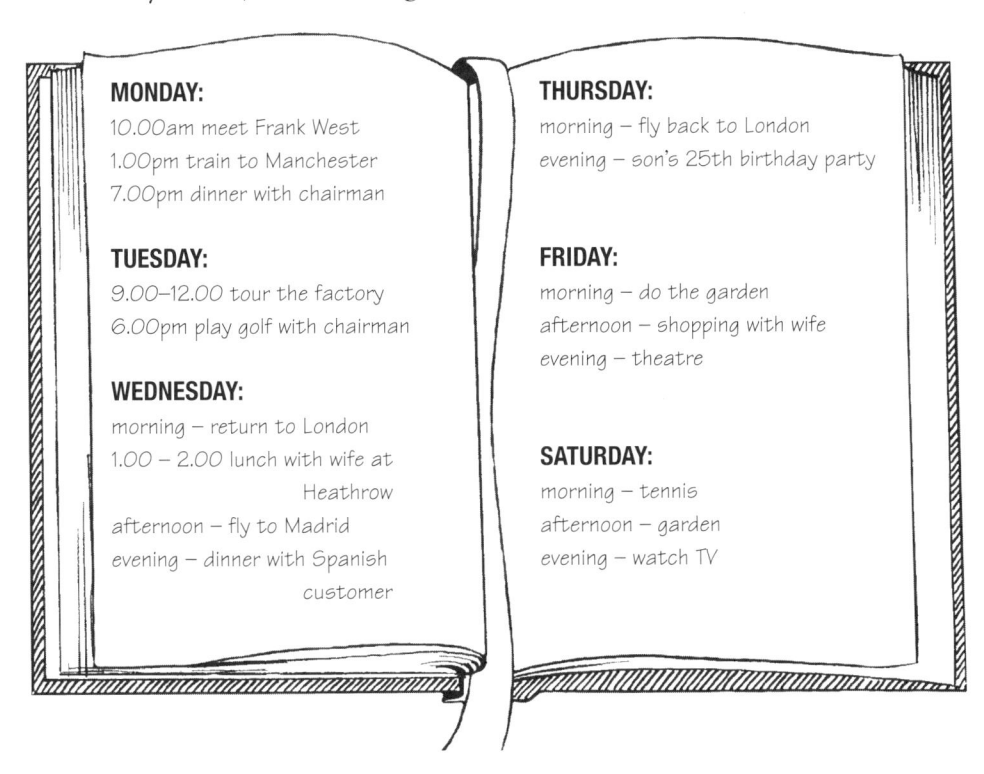

MONDAY:
10.00am meet Frank West
1.00pm train to Manchester
7.00pm dinner with chairman

TUESDAY:
9.00–12.00 tour the factory
6.00pm play golf with chairman

WEDNESDAY:
morning – return to London
1.00 – 2.00 lunch with wife at Heathrow
afternoon – fly to Madrid
evening – dinner with Spanish customer

THURSDAY:
morning – fly back to London
evening – son's 25th birthday party

FRIDAY:
morning – do the garden
afternoon – shopping with wife
evening – theatre

SATURDAY:
morning – tennis
afternoon – garden
evening – watch TV

B Working in pairs, choose the use of the Present Simple in the following sentences. Write letters a–c in the boxes.

a = official time   **b** = fixed date   **c** = after *if* or a time conjunction

1. I get to Rome at 2pm.
2. The school holidays start on 30th June.
3. The English class finishes at 7.
4. Registration day for the computer course is next Tuesday.
5. When they get the money, they'll buy a new car.
6. If the train is on time, Chris will be here by 7 o'clock.
7. Will you check the business contract before you go home this evening?
8. How many of us will have a job after the new boss looks at the company's poor performance?
9. I'll tell you everything as soon as I can.
10. The party is on Saturday.

Teacher's notes

Conclusion (10 minutes)

Activity C The students in pairs complete the dialogue. If there is time, there should be the opportunity for some of them to act out the dialogue.

Homework

Activity D Students complete the activity by choosing the correct form of the verb.

Key

C 1 are helping 2 get 3 start/are starting 4 is having
   5 are you doing 6 is coming 7 are flying 8 get
   9 gets 10 are having

D 1 leaves (a) 2 is coming (d) 3 starts (a) 4 opens (c)
   5 is (b) 6 feed (a) 7 is taking (d) 8 are having (d)
   9 is (c) 10 is giving (d)

29 Use of present tenses to express the future (continued)

C Complete the sentences by putting the verbs in brackets into the correct form: Present Continuous or Present Simple.

Geoff: Hi, Dan. Will you and Jill come on the river with us on Saturday?

Dan: Sorry, Geoff, we can't. We (1 help).............................. Jill's brother install his new kitchen.

Geoff: That's a lot of hard work.

Dan: I know. And it's a waste of time. He won't be ready when we (2 get).............................. there. He'll still be in bed while we (3 start).............................. organizing things. He (4 have).............................. a party on Friday night.

Geoff: Perhaps he won't go to bed.

Dan: Perhaps. What (5 do you).............................. the following weekend?

Geoff: Carrie's sister (6 come)........................... . She wants to see the museum.

Dan: And then we (7 fly).............................. to Greece for our holiday.

Geoff: We'll have to do it when you (8 get).............................. back.

Dan: It'll be September then. It (9 get).............................. cold in September.

Geoff: And, in any case, Carrie and I (10 have).............................. our holiday then. Next year?

Dan: OK.

D Complete the sentences by putting the verb in the correct form. Give the reason for your choice by writing a–d in the boxes.

a = official time   b = fixed date   c = after *if* or a time conjunction
d = definite plan

☐ 1 Come along! Hurry up! The train (leave) .... at four o'clock.

☐ 2 Matt (come) .... to stay at the weekend.

☐ 3 The play (start) .... at 7.30.

☐ 4 Will you finish that painting before the exhibition (open) ....?

☐ 5 The General Election (be) .... on 9th June.

☐ 6 They (feed) .... the elephants at 10 o'clock.

☐ 7 The government (take) .... delivery of the new fighter planes in September.

☐ 8 We (have) .... a special ceremony to mark the occasion.

☐ 9 I'll kill him if he (be) .... late again.

☐ 10 She (give) .... her parrot to a friend during the holidays.

Teacher's notes

30 Short answers with *so* or *neither/nor*

Aim	To show how to use short answers to express agreement.
Preparation	Copy the handouts on pages 107 and 109 – one copy per student.

Introduction *(5 minutes)*

Begin by asking students to write down:
- their favourite food
- their favourite TV programme
- where they would like to go for a holiday
- an actor (male or female) they don't like
- something they didn't like when they were younger

Then take the lists from three or four of the students. After looking at them, tell the class about one of the students whose list you have. For example:
Laura likes pizza. Does anyone else like pizza?
If several students claim they do, do your response in two parts:
i) *Ah, Laura likes pizza and so does Tessa.*
ii) *Ah, Laura likes pizza and so do Tessa and Mark.*
Put these two statements on the board. Now look at one of the other lists and tell the class, for example:
Sara likes Tom Cruise.
Then look round the class to see if anyone agrees. When a student indicates that s/he does, prompt him/her to say: *So do I.*
Repeat this with another example taken from the lists.

Presentation *(15 minutes)*

Explain that you use short answers such as those with *so* to show the situation is the same for someone or something. Write examples on the board.

I like Rio. – So does Margarita.
Bethany is at university in the USA. – So are Nick and Lizzie.
My old car used a lot of petrol. – So did mine.
Jack has gone to Cuba on holiday. – So has Alice.
I must study harder next year. – So must I.

Highlight the form on the board:
So + auxiliary or modal + subject
Now explain that we use *neither* or *nor* in the same way to show the situation is the same for someone or something but when we are referring to something negative.
I haven't seen Petra for weeks. – Nor have I.
Sally can't speak Polish. – Neither can Tony.
Show the form on the board:
Nor/Neither + auxiliary or modal + subject
Point out that although the agreement is about something negative, the verb is still positive. Also tell them that both *neither* and *nor* are possible, but we usually use *nor*.
Give back to the students their lists of favourite food, etc. They work in pairs. Set up the following dialogue:
A *Do you/Would you ...?* (for example: *Do you like cheese? Would you like to go to Florida?*)
B *Yes.* or *No.*
A *So do/would I.* or *Nor do/would I.*
They act out this dialogue for 5 minutes.

Practice *(20 minutes)*

Activity A Students work in pairs. This can be competitive to see which pair finishes first.

Activity B Students work in small groups. They have to see how many examples they can get within a specified time – probably 5 minutes or less. You must have time to hear the examples.

Conclusion *(10 minutes)*

Activity C Students work individually. Check orally.

(continued on page 108)

Key

A 1 e 2 i 3 b 4 f 5 h 6 a 7 d 8 j 9 c 10 g
B *Possible answers (there are many more):*
   Japan isn't in Europe. Nor is Ecuador.
   Ecuador has fewer than 12 million people. So does Sweden.
   Japan is a monarchy. So are Sweden and Spain.
   Sweden is bigger than Japan. So is Spain.
   Ecuador isn't an island. Nor is Sweden.
C 1 can 2 is 3 was 4 is 5 would 6 is 7 does 8 has 9 must 10 did

(continued on page 108)

30 Short answers with *so* or *neither/nor*

A Match the sentences with the correct response.

1 David works late on Tuesdays.
2 I've never been to Turkey.
3 Mary's sure she'll get the job.
4 Bob couldn't swim.
5 Alice's team lost their game.
6 Jean's bought a new car.
7 Alec would like to win the lottery.
8 Mozambique was damaged by floods.
9 Debbie can't afford a new computer.
10 Cameron won't be at work this week.

a So has Dan.
b So is Pete.
c Nor can her husband.
d So would I.
e So does Matt.
f Nor could Jane.
g Nor will Margaret.
h So did mine.
i Nor has Ruth.
j So was Bangladesh.

B How many sentence pairs you can make from the table below? For example: *Sweden is in Europe. So is Spain.*

JAPAN	SWEDEN	ECUADOR	SPAIN
Asia	Europe	South America	Europe
island	mid-continent	mid-continent	mid-continent
Japanese	Swedish	Spanish	Spanish
+377,000 sq m	+449,000 sq m	+270,000 sq m	+504,000 sq m
125m people	8m people	11m people	39m people
monarchy	monarchy	republic	monarchy

C Complete the responses in brackets.

1 We can't have our holidays in July this year. (Neither .... Lauren and Jack.)
2 Germany is a federal state. (So .... the USA.)
3 The Masons' house was damaged in the storm. (So .... the Palmers'.)
4 Ethiopia is a very poor country. (So .... Mali.)
5 Pete wouldn't like to work in a foreign country. (Nor .... Ivan.)
6 My birth sign is Taurus. (So .... Harriet's.)
7 The rain in Spain stays mainly in the plain. (So .... the rain in Argentina.)
8 Diane has got her pilot's licence. (So .... Ryan.)
9 Mike must pass the exam in July. (So .... Dave.)
10 I didn't hear the news until yesterday evening. (Nor .... I.)

Teacher's notes

Homework

Activity D Students complete the dialogue at home. Get some students to act it out in the next lesson.

Key

D 1 have I   2 is mine   3 can mine   4 did we
   5 did mine/my boyfriend   6 is mine   7 does mine
   8 is mine   9 does mine   10 will I

30 Short answers with *so* or *neither/nor*
(continued)

D Complete the dialogue by giving the correct response.

Jane: I've got a new boyfriend.

Tina: That's funny. So (1)..............................

Jane: Mine's very good-looking.

Tina: So (2)..............................

Jane: The problem is that he can't drive.

Tina: Neither (3)..............................

Jane: We went to the theatre last week.

Tina: So (4).............................. But he didn't like the play.

Jane: Nor (5).............................. He said he'd seen it before.

Tina: Then why did he go again?

Jane: I wanted to see it. My new boyfriend's very thoughtful.

Tina: So (6).............................. He doesn't like to upset me.

Jane: Nor (7).............................. What's his name? Mine's called Tim.

Tina: So (8).............................. How old is he?

Jane: 26. He looks like Leonardo di Caprio.

Tina: So (9).............................. Do you think ...?

Jane: I'll never see him again.

Tina: Nor (10)..............................

Vocabulary: Lessons 31–40

31 Character and personality adjectives

Aim	To introduce and practise a number of adjectives, both positive and negative, to describe people's character and personality.
Preparation	Copy the handout on page 111 – one copy per student.

Introduction (5 minutes)

Introduce the subject of adjectives to describe character and personality by referring to astrology and star signs:
Does anyone believe in astrology? I'm not sure I do, really. My star sign is Sagittarius, which according to astrology means that my good points are that I'm optimistic and honest. On the other hand I have some bad points too – I'm supposed to be impatient and argumentative. Then there's my sister. Her star sign is Gemini. Her good points are that she's charming and versatile while her bad points are that she's restless and impractical. What about you? What are your good and bad points?
Write the following on the board:
My good/bad points are that I'm ____ and ____.
Now get the class to work with a partner and to take it in turns to talk about their good points and bad points using the above pattern. Ask one or two students to tell you about the person they spoke to.

Presentation (15 minutes)

Explain that today you are going to look at some common adjectives to describe people's character and personality.

Activity A This is a good way to check how much the students already know. Read through the instructions. Do the first example with the whole class then let them work through the other examples on their own in pairs. Check orally, paying particular attention to any words that were new or unfamiliar.

Practice (20 minutes)

Activity B This activity introduces a number of other adjectives, plus the ones in Activity A. Again, let them work through this in pairs. Check orally. Try not to give 'moral' judgements regarding positive and negative characteristics, since many of these may be culture-based. As a quick follow-up, get them to choose three adjectives from their positive list and three from their negative list and to rate them 1–3 as the best/worst characteristics to have.

Activity C This is a revision activity to give the students a chance to use the above words. Arrange the class into groups of three or four students. Each person takes it in turns to read out a question then to give their opinion. The others can naturally join in and give theirs too. To make sure they don't spend too long on any one question, after a few minutes encourage them to move on to the next question: *Right, go on to the next question now!*

Conclusion (10 minutes)

Activity D This is a simple test to see if they have remembered the words practised. Each student works on his/her own. Check orally.

Homework

To write their own sentences using eight of the above adjectives.

Key

A 1 c 2 i 3 f 4 h 5 a 6 d 7 j 8 b 9 g 10 e
B *Possible answer:*
POSITIVE: ambitious, brave, cheerful, confident, friendly, generous, honest, kind, patient, punctual, reliable, sensitive
NEGATIVE: big-headed, boring, bossy, dishonest, envious, impatient, jealous, lazy, mean, rude, selfish, shy, stubborn
D 1 shy 2 bossy 3 lazy 4 stubborn 5 jealous 6 ambitious 7 confident 8 envious 9 honest 10 mean

31 Character and personality adjectives

A Match up the following. (Look at the example.)

1. Ambitious people ...
2. Brave people ...
3. Cheerful people ...
4. Dishonest people ...
5. Honest people ...
6. Lazy people ...
7. Mean people ...
8. Punctual people ...
9. Rude people ...
10. Selfish people ...

a. never cheat.
b. are never late.
c. want to be successful.
d. dislike hard work.
e. only think of themselves.
f. are always happy.
g. have no manners.
h. often lie.
i. are not easily frightened.
j. don't like spending money.

1	2	3	4	5	6	7	8	9	10
c									

B Work in pairs. Arrange these adjectives under three headings – **positive**, **negative** and **not sure**.

ambitious big-headed boring bossy
brave cheerful confident dishonest
envious friendly generous honest
impatient jealous kind lazy mean
patient punctual reliable rude
selfish sensitive shy stubborn

POSITIVE	NEGATIVE	NOT SURE

C Work in groups. Discuss the following.

1. Who is the *meanest* person you have met? Give an example of how he/she was mean. Who is the most *generous* person you have met? Again, give an example of this person's generosity.
2. If you want to be considered *polite* in your country, what sort of things should you do? What sort of behaviour would be considered *rude*?
3. Are you ever *envious* of people with lots of money? What other things can make people envious?
4. Name five jobs where you have to be very *patient*.
5. How *brave* are you? Which of the following would you do?
   a Hold a large snake.
   b Spend the night alone in a haunted house.
   c Do a bungee jump.
6. Are men more *ambitious* than women or are today's women more *ambitious* than men? Give reasons.

D Which type of people might say the following things? How would you describe them?

1. I hate going to parties and meeting new people.
2. Do the washing up, and when you've finished that you can do the hoovering!
3. I've got lots to do today, but I think I'll just watch TV instead.
4. Once I've made up my mind, nothing will make me change it!
5. If you look at my girlfriend again I'm going to hit you!
6. One day I'm going to be Prime Minister!
7. Give me a chance to do the job! I know I can do it!
8. My neighbours are off to Hawaii tomorrow for a month. It's all right for some people, isn't it?
9. Does this £10 note belong to anybody? I found it on the floor.
10. No, you can't have a sweet, they're mine! Buy your own!

Teacher's notes

32 Words that sound the same (homophones)

Aim	To check that students know the differences between pairs of words that sound the same but are spelt differently and have different meanings.
Preparation	Copy the handouts on pages 113 and 115 – one copy per student. Cut up the handout on page 115.

Introduction *(5 minutes)*

Dictate the following two sentences:
'Smoking is not allowed!' he said aloud.
I know a great place for catching plaice.
Write the sentences on the board. How many students wrote them correctly? Ask one or two to explain the differences between *allowed/aloud* and *place/plaice*. Tell them that words like this – that sound alike but are spelt differently and have different meanings – are called homophones. Tell them that in this lesson you're going to be looking at various homophones.

Presentation *(20 minutes)*

Activities A and B Introduce Activity A. Go through the example (0), then let them do the activity in pairs. Check orally and explain any new words. Do the same with Activity B. Again check orally. Ask the students which word pairs the pictures illustrate.

(continued on page 114)

Key

A 1 write 2 peak 3 hare 4 peace 5 steel 6 fare
  7 pane 8 bored 9 flour 10 cheep

B 1 dye 2 pear 3 scent 4 cell 5 tale 6 fur 7 dear
  8 plaice 9 stairs 10 alter

(continued on page 114)

32 Words that sound the same (homophones)

A Write down the missing words.

	sounds like ...	means ...	word
0	meet	You eat it.	**meat**
1	right	You do it with a pen.	
2	peek	The top of a mountain.	
3	hair	An animal.	
4	piece	Not war.	
5	steal	A metal.	
6	fair	The money you pay to travel.	
7	pain	The glass in a window.	
8	board	Not interested.	
9	flower	You use it for baking.	
10	cheap	Sound a bird makes.	

B Underline the correct answer.

1 Which word means *to change the colour of something*?   die   dye
2 Which word is a fruit?   pair   pear
3 Which word is to do with smells?   scent   cent
4 Which word is a room in a prison?   sell   cell
5 Which word is a story?   tale   tail
6 Which word can be a coat?   fir   fur
7 Which word means *expensive*?   deer   dear
8 Which word is a type of fish?   plaice   place
9 Which word is part of a house?   stares   stairs
10 Which word means *to change*?   alter   altar

Teacher's notes

Practice *(15 minutes)*

Activity C The students, working in small groups (three or four students), now try their own hand at writing similar activities. Half the groups are 1s and half are 2s. Give Group 1s their pairs of words and tell them to write an activity similar to Activity A. Give Group 2s their pairs of words and tell them to write an activity similar to Activity B.

When they have finished, Group 1s and Group 2s swap papers and see if they can do the activity that has been set. Go around and listen, offering help when needed. The groups write down their answers on a piece of paper, then pass them to the original group for correcting.

Conclusion *(10 minutes)*

Activity D Give out the letter and get the students, working in pairs, to correct it. Tell them there are 27 words wrongly used. Check orally. Explain any new words.

Homework

To write sentences showing the differences in meaning between the following pairs of words. (Write them up on the board.)
plain–plane
bolder–boulder
cymbal–symbol
sight–site
flea–flee

Key

D *In this order:*
road, know, sell, dear, sale, find, fair, made, profit, see, been, stairs, great, sea, plain, veil, tears, weather, rain, mist, I'll, ring, meet, would, dyed, time, alter

32 Words that sound the same (homophones) *(continued)*

C Group 1

Write an activity similar to Activity A. Use these pairs of words:

great–grate
meet–meat
vale–veil
route–root
see–sea
vain–vein

C Group 2

Write an activity similar to Activity B. Use these pairs of words:

bow–bough
course–coarse
heal–heel
missed–mist
sail–sale
sew–sow

D

12A Grange Rode
Sunderland

June 1st

Dear Janet,

I don't no if Paula told you or not, but we had to cell our house. When Bob lost his job it became too deer for us to keep. It was for sail for ages but we finally managed to fined a buyer. We got a fare price for it and even maid a small prophet. So we rent a flat now (sea above address). We've bean here for just over a month and we like it. It's on the ground floor so there aren't any stares to climb. We also have a grate view of the see from our balcony. By the way, Susan is getting married in July. She's bought a fabulous wedding dress. It's plane with a long vale. (I expect her mother will shed a few tiers at the wedding!)

The whether has been terrible lately, hasn't it? Nothing but reign and missed! Anyway, Janet, I'd better stop now. But isle give you a wring soon. We really must meat up before Janet's wedding. Bob and the children wood love to see you again.

Love,

Sally

ps You may not recognize me now as I've died my hair jet black! I felt it was thyme to altar my appearance again.

Teacher's notes

33 How are you? How do you feel?

Aim	To teach and practise some adjectives that describe how people are or feel.
Preparation	Copy the handout on page 117 – one copy per student.

Introduction (5 minutes)

Introduce the subject by saying (and acting out) one of the following. Make up your own reasons, if more appropriate.
I'm feeling really excited today because (tonight I'm going to a Ricky Martin concert).
I'm feeling really upset today because (my cat was run over last night).
I'm feeling really disappointed today because (a manuscript for a short story I'd sent off to a publisher came back).
Now write the following on the board and ask the students for possible ways to finish them off.
I'm feeling very happy today because ...
I'm feeling very sad today because ...

Presentation (20 minutes)

Activity A The students work in pairs. Give each pair a copy of the handout. They match up the sentence halves. Check orally.

Practice (15 minutes)

Activity B Give each student a copy of the handout. Working alone, they complete each sentence in their own words. When they have finished, they find a partner and compare answers.

Conclusion (10 minutes)

This is a listening exercise to check some of the words learnt during the lesson. Tell the students to write down the numbers 1–8 on a separate piece of paper. Then read out the following sentences, allowing time for the students to write down their answers.

1 We were so __(bleep!)__ during the politician's speech that we almost fell asleep.
2 When she moved from Britain to France, she felt very __(bleep!)__ at first. She missed everything – especially her family and friends.
3 They were all __(bleep!)__ when they heard that James had won a national Talent Competition. No one even knew that he could sing.
4 I am very __(bleep!)__ today after all that singing we did last night.
5 We all felt very __(bleep!)__ when we heard that Sally had won £20,000 plus a free trip to Australia and New Zealand.
6 She felt very __(bleep!)__ when her father started singing in front of her friends. He was so out of tune!
7 The students were all feeling __(bleep!)__ as they waited for their exam results.
8 Peter was very __(bleep!)__ when they offered the job to someone else. It was just the sort of job he had always wanted.

Check orally.

Homework

To write their own sentences (as in Activity B) for the following adjectives. (Write them up on the board.)
happy
depressed
tired
angry
disgusted
stiff
fed up
restless

Key

A 1 e 2 j 3 n 4 c 5 r 6 h 7 l 8 q 9 a 10 o
 11 f 12 k 13 p 14 b 15 m 16 g 17 d 18 i

Conclusion
1 bored 2 homesick 3 amazed 4 hoarse
5 envious 6 embarrassed 7 tense/nervous/worried
8 disappointed/upset

33 How are you? How do you feel?

A Match up the sentence halves. Write your answers in the boxes below.

1 She was disappointed ...
2 The children were excited ...
3 Cathy felt dizzy ...
4 They were hoarse ...
5 Mrs Brown was relieved ...
6 My sister was very upset ...
7 Paula felt envious ...
8 Clive was very confused ...
9 They were exhausted ...
10 The parents were worried ...
11 We were bored ...
12 Susan felt very homesick ...
13 The boxer was unconscious for several minutes ...
14 Most people were amazed ...
15 The manager became suspicious ...
16 The passengers were annoyed ...
17 She felt embarrassed ...
18 Tom felt tense ...

a after running in the London Marathon.
b when France beat Brazil to win the World Cup, because there were so many great Brazilian players.
c after shouting at the football match.
d when she slipped and fell in the middle of the crowded supermarket.
e when she failed her driving test.
f with the film and left before the end.
g when they announced that the train would be 30 minutes late.
h when her dog died.
i as he sat waiting to see the dentist.
j at going to the circus.
k when she first moved to Greece on her own.
l of her brother's success.
m when he saw the man hovering in the staff cloakroom.
n looking down from the high building.
o when their daughter was late coming home.
p when his opponent gave him a right hook to the chin.
q when he first drove on the right.
r to find out it wasn't cancer.

1	2	3	4	5	6	7	8	9	10	11	12	13	14	15	16	17	18

B Complete the following in your own words.

1 I was very disappointed when ...
2 As a child I used to get very excited when ...
3 The last time I was hoarse was because ...
4 I was very upset when ...
5 I sometimes feel envious of ...
6 I felt very confused ...
7 I was really exhausted ...
8 I was really worried once when ...
9 A film/TV programme/book (choose) that made me feel really bored was ...
10 I was amazed when ...
11 I get very suspicious ...
12 The last time I got annoyed was when ...
13 The first time I felt homesick was when ...
14 I would feel very embarrassed if ...
15 I sometimes get tense ...

Teacher's notes

34 Phrasal verbs with *out*

Aim	To teach and practise some common phrasal verbs with out (*break out, come out,* etc.).
Preparation	Copy the handouts on pages 119 and 121 – one copy per student. Cut up the handout on page 121.

Introduction *(5 minutes)*

Introduce the subject by writing the following on the board:
A *Why did you let the fire go out?*
B *Because I had to go out.*
Ask the students if they can explain the differences between the two uses of *go out* in the above dialogue. (A = *be extinguished*; B = *leave the house and go somewhere else*.) Ask them if they know what this sort of verb is called in English. Write on the board: *phrasal verb*. Ask if they know any other phrasal verbs with *out*. Write any suggestions on the board. Then tell the students that you're going to look at examples of phrasal verbs with *out* in today's lesson.

Presentation *(15 minutes)*

Activity A Give out the first handout. Let the students work in pairs. They match the verbs with the definitions. Check orally, then let them test each other by taking it in turns to read out a definition and see if their partner can give the correct phrasal verb.

Practice *(25 minutes)*

Activity B Again, working in pairs they sort out the sentence halves. If there is time, as before they could test each other by covering up the answers, then one student reading one of the openings from column 1 while his/her partner answers with the correct ending from column 2.

(continued on page 120)

Key

A 1 e 2 i 3 o 4 l 5 h 6 d 7 k 8 a 9 f 10 n
 11 b 12 j 13 p 14 c 15 m 16 g
B 1 d 2 l 3 p 4 h 5 n 6 j 7 e 8 a 9 k 10 m
 11 b 12 f 13 o 14 i 15 c 16 g

(continued on page 120)

34 Phrasal verbs with *out*

A Match the phrasal verbs in column 1 with the correct definitions in column 2. Write your answers in the boxes below.

1
1 break out
2 come out
3 drop out (of)
4 fall out
5 find out
6 knock out
7 leave out
8 Look out!
9 make out
10 pass out
11 pull out
12 put out
13 run out
14 set out
15 turn out
16 wear out

2
a Be careful! (*warning*)
b (*of a vehicle*) move out of a line of traffic
c begin a journey
d eliminate from a competition
e start and spread (*e.g. a war, a disease*)
f manage to see, read or understand something
g become unusable because of continuous use
h discover something by making enquiries
i (*of a book, magazine*) be published
j extinguish a fire, flames, etc.
k fail to include something or someone
l quarrel
m produce, manufacture
n faint, lose consciousness
o withdraw, especially from academic studies
p expire (*e.g. a passport*)

1	2	3	4	5	6	7	8	9	10	11	12	13	14	15	16

B Match up the sentence halves in columns 1 and 2. Write your answers in the boxes below.

1
1 John hasn't spoken to Jill since they ...
2 When both his parents died, he had to ...
3 She had to brake sharply when a car suddenly ...
4 There's a car coming! ...
5 I need a new pair of shoes. These are ...
6 The Second World War ...
7 My passport ...
8 None of the runners wanted to wear the number 13, so they ...
9 I'll go and collect him if I can ...
10 How many cars does the factory ...
11 His new book ...
12 It was so hot and stuffy that several people ...
13 Because of the traffic, we decided to ...
14 What does that sign say? I can't ...
15 In the 1998 World Cup, Croatia ...
16 It took fire fighters eight hours to ...

2
a left it out.
b comes out tomorrow.
c were knocked out by France in the semi-final.
d fell out last week.
e runs out in January.
f passed out.
g put out the blaze.
h Look out!
i make it out without my glasses.
j broke out in 1939 when Germany invaded Poland.
k find out what time his plane arrives.
l drop out of university so that he could look after his young sisters.
m turn out each week?
n completely worn out.
o set out early.
p pulled out in front of her.

1	2	3	4	5	6	7	8	9	10	11	12	13	14	15	16

From *Instant Lessons 2 Intermediate* edited by Peter Watcyn-Jones © Penguin Books 2000

Teacher's notes

Activity C Students work in pairs – Student 1 and Student 2. Give everyone a copy of the appropriate handout. They now see if they can remember the verbs they have been practising, by trying to suggest the missing verbs from the sentences.

Conclusion *(5 minutes)*

Activity D Students work individually. Give each one a copy of the handout. Tell them they have to rewrite each sentence using phrasal verbs they have learnt today. Check orally.

Homework

Students use their dictionaries to find five other phrasal verbs. Ask them to write sentences of their own using each one.

Key

D 1 This insurance policy has run out.
   2 When did the Falklands War break out?
   3 Isabel Allende's new novel came out last week.
   4 No one understood why he decided to drop out of school before he had any qualifications.
   5 My parents and I are always falling out.
   6 At least ten people passed out in the heat.
   7 What time shall we set out?
   8 How many bicycles does this factory turn out each year?
   9 Would you like me to find out when the next train leaves for Brighton?
   10 It is often very difficult to put out a forest fire.

34 Phrasal verbs with *out* (continued)

C Student 1

Read each sentence to your partner and ask him/her for the missing verbs. Give 2 points for the correct verb and the correct tense and 1 point for the correct verb but the wrong tense.

1. Manchester United were _____ out in the semi-final of the European Cup.
2. Your handwriting is terrible! I can hardly _____ it out.
3. My uncle was working in Kuwait when the Gulf War _____ out.
4. We _____ out at 10.30 in the morning and didn't arrive until 5.30 in the afternoon.
5. I must renew my television licence. It _____ out at the end of this month.
6. How long did it take them to _____ out the fire?
7. I'm not surprised they got divorced. They were always _____ out, weren't they?
8. They were such boring lessons that half the class _____ out before the exams.

Key: *1 knocked 2 make 3 broke 4 set 5 runs 6 put 7 falling 8 dropped*

Who scored more points?

C Student 2

Read each sentence to your partner and ask him/her for the missing verbs. Give 2 points for the correct verb and the correct tense and 1 point for the correct verb but the wrong tense.

1. The accident was caused by a car which suddenly _____ out in front of him.
2. This factory _____ out over a thousand vacuum cleaners every week.
3. The stadium was so hot and humid that several of the spectators _____ out.
4. The new music magazine *Classical Gas* _____ out tomorrow.
5. Since he was injured, we had to _____ him out of the team.
6. _____ out! There's a bull in that field!
7. This is the second pair of football boots my son has _____ out this year.
8. Just wait here while I _____ out what time the last bus goes.

Key: *1 pulled 2 turns 3 passed 4 comes 5 leave 6 Look 7 worn 8 find*

Who scored more points?

D Rewrite the following sentences using a suitable phrasal verb.

1. This insurance policy is out of date.
2. When did the Falklands War start?
3. Isabel Allende's new novel was published last week.
4. No one understood why he decided to leave school before he had any qualifications.
5. My parents and I are always quarrelling.
6. At least ten people fainted in the heat.
7. What time shall we start our journey?
8. How many bicycles does this factory produce each year?
9. Would you like me to get some information about when the next train leaves for Brighton?
10. It is often very difficult to extinguish a forest fire.

Teacher's notes

35 Words and phrases with *make* and *do*

Aim	To teach and practise some common words and phrases with *make* or *do*.
Preparation	Copy and cut up the handout on page 123 – one copy per pair. Copy the handout on page 125 – one copy per student.

Introduction *(5 minutes)*

Introduce the subject by saying, for example: *I've had a really busy weekend. On Saturday morning, for example, I did the shopping, did the hoovering, and even made all the beds. Then I made lunch and did some gardening for a few hours. I was really tired when I finished, so I made myself a nice cup of tea and watched TV for the rest of the evening.*
Write on the board the two headings:
MAKE   DO
Ask the students if they can remember anything you did or made on Saturday. Write them under the correct heading. Ask the students if they know any other phrases with *make* or *do*. Write these up too.

Presentation *(15 minutes)*

Activity A Let the students work in pairs. Give each pair a copy of the handout. Tell them to decide which words go with *make* and which words go with *do*. Check orally. Finally, to practise, let the students test each other. One student looks at the handout while the other answers. The first student reads out a word/phrase from the list and his/her partner says whether it is *make* or *do*. When they have done about five, they change roles and do it again.

Practice *(25 minutes)*

Activity B Students work in pairs – Student 1 and Student 2. Give everyone a copy of the appropriate handout. They now see how many of the words and phrases they remember, by trying to suggest the missing forms of *make* or *do*.

(continued on page 124)

Key

A an excuse (M)   a mistake (M)   research (D)
an appointment (M)   the washing-up (D)
friends (M)   a good job (D)   one's hair (D)
a noise (M)   a speech (M)   homework (D)
one's duty (D)   a complaint (M)   business (D)
an effort (M)   harm (D)   one's best (D)
a journey (M)   an examination (D)
fun of someone (M)   a fuss (M)   an exercise (D)
a lot of money (M)   someone a favour (D)

(continued on page 124)

35 Words and phrases with *make* and *do*

A The following words and phrases are used with *make* or *do*. Write M (for *make*) or D (for *do*) next to each one.

an excuse	a good job	a complaint	an examination
a mistake	one's hair	business	fun of someone
research	a noise	an effort	a fuss
an appointment	a speech	harm	an exercise
the washing-up	homework	one's best	a lot of money
friends	one's duty	a journey	someone a favour

B Student 1

Read out the following sentences and ask your partner for the missing verbs. Give 2 points for the correct verb and the correct tense; give 1 point for the correct verb but the wrong tense. You start.

1. Good morning, I'd like to _____ an appointment with Dr Brown, please.
2. If I cook, will you _____ the washing-up?
3. Could you _____ me a favour, John? Could you post this letter for me on your way home?
4. If you want to pass your exams this summer you'll have to _____ a far greater effort than now.
5. I can't come out tonight. I've got to stay in and _____ my hair.
6. Last week we _____ a very difficult exercise on prepositions.
7. Stop _____ such a noise! I'm trying to sleep!
8. Most people get nervous when asked to _____ a speech.
9. Everyone knows that smoking _____ you harm.
10. People often used to _____ fun of him because he was so fat.
11. Children should _____ their duty and look after their parents when they are old.
12. My grandparents always _____ a big fuss of me whenever I go and visit them.

Key: *1 make 2 do 3 do 4 make 5 do 6 did 7 making 8 make 9 does 10 make 11 do 12 make*

Who scored more points?

B Student 2

Read out the following sentences and ask your partner for the missing verbs. Give 2 points for the correct verb and the correct tense; give 1 point for the correct verb but the wrong tense. Your partner starts.

1. Could I see the manager, please? I wish to _____ a complaint.
2. Our company _____ business with lots of foreign companies.
3. Whenever I'm asked to do something, I always try to _____ a good job.
4. My son is at Cambridge University _____ research.
5. Do you find it easy or difficult to _____ friends?
6. The only way of _____ a lot of money in this country is to win it on the National Lottery.
7. Many students are afraid to speak English because they don't like to _____ mistakes.
8. I forgot to _____ my homework last night.
9. They _____ a very long journey from London to Nepal.
10. I'm _____ the Cambridge First Certificate exam in the summer.
11. The teacher wished the students good luck for their exam and told them to _____ their best.
12. He didn't really feel like going to the party, so he _____ an excuse about not feeling well.

Key: *1 make 2 does 3 do 4 doing 5 make 6 making 7 make 8 do 9 made 10 doing 11 do 12 made*

Who scored more points?

From *Instant Lessons 2 Intermediate* edited by Peter Watcyn-Jones © Penguin Books 2000

Teacher's notes

Activity C Students work in pairs. Give each pair a copy of the handout. Explain that the text contains a number of mistakes. They try to find them. Check orally.

Conclusion (5 minutes)

Write the following on the board:
1 The best way to _____ a lot of money is ...
2 The last time I _____ someone a favour was ...
3 If I had to _____ an excuse for not _____ my homework, I'd say ...
4 One occasion when you _____ a speech is ...
5 I would love to _____ research on ...

Students work in pairs. They choose their own endings and also put in the correct forms of *make* and *do*. Check orally with one or two students.

Homework

Students make up their own sentences for the following:
make an impression
do good
make progress
do wrong

Key

C *10 mistakes as follows:*
does a lot of business ... made a journey ... doing research ... doing the washing-up ... make a speech ... made an excuse ... done a lot of favours ... do a good job ... do me any harm ... make too many mistakes

Conclusion
1 make   2 did   3 make, doing   4 make   5 do

35 Words and phrases with *make* and *do*
(continued)

C Find the mistakes in the following text. (They are all to do with *make* or *do*.)

My friend James works for a computer company that makes a lot of business with Sweden. So last April they sent him there for six weeks. He made friends with a man called Henrik and together they did a journey to the north of the country where they met a man called Gustav Löfgren, a man who had made a lot of money from writing children's books. He had a daughter, Ulla, who was making research at Umeå University. One day while they were making the washing-up together, James asked Ulla to marry him. At first she thought he was making fun of her but when she saw that he was serious, she agreed.

That was back in April. The wedding is going to be in September and James has asked me to be his best man. I'm not looking forward to it, as it means having to do a speech. But as James is my best friend, I suppose I'll just have to make an effort to overcome my nervousness. And he wouldn't really believe me if I did an excuse not to go to his wedding. Besides, he's made a lot of favours for me in the past and he seems to think I'll make a good job. Well, speaking in public can't really make me any harm, can it? But I think I'll make an appointment with my doctor to get some tranquillizers, just in case. I know I'll be nervous even if I take pills, but I'm determined to do my best. I just hope I don't do too many mistakes on the big day.

Teacher's notes

36 Pairs of words that are often confused

Aim	To look at pairs of words that students often mix up, such as *continual/continuous*, *lend/borrow*, etc.
Preparation	Copy the handouts on pages 127 and 129 – one copy per student.

Introduction *(5 minutes)*

Write the following on the board:
My brother is an electric/electrical engineer.
I've just bought a new electric/electrical kettle.
Ask the students to choose the correct words for the above (*electrical engineer*, *electric kettle*) and to try to explain the difference. For example:
If your brother was an electric engineer, he'd be live – you'd get a shock when you touched him.
Electric is used of things that produce electricity or are worked by electricity. *Electrical* is used of people and their work or in such phrases as:
There's an electrical fault in the system.
Ask for more examples using *electric* or *electrical* (*electric train, shaver, drill, lawn mower, light, blanket*; *electrical engineering, apparatus, fault*).
Tell the students that in this lesson you are going to be looking at pairs of words like this that can be confusing.

Presentation *(25 minutes)*

Activity A Let the students work in pairs. Give everyone a copy of the handout. Do the first example with the whole class, then let them complete the others. Check orally, giving explanations as required:

1 *To lend* is to give something to someone else for a short time. *To borrow* is to get something from someone else for a short time.
2 *To rise* means to go up or move upwards (prices, the sun in the sky, etc.) It has no direct object. If you *raise* something, you make it higher. It has a direct object.
3 *To rob* is to steal from a house, shop, bank, etc. *To steal* is a general word which means to take something that doesn't belong to you.
4 *To lie* means, in this context, to be situated – *Swansea is situated to the west of Cardiff*. *To lay* the table means to prepare it for eating by placing a tablecloth, knives and forks, etc. on it.
5 When you *wink* you deliberately close then open just one eye. When you *blink*, you close then open both eyes – often mechanically.
6 *Continuous* describes things that go on without a break (e.g. continuous/non-stop performances). *Continual* describes separate, often annoying, actions which are repeated over a period of time (e.g. continual interruptions) or continuing for a long time without stopping (e.g. continual rain).
7 *Space* here means empty space between two things. *Room* means enough space for a particular purpose (room in the car, fridge, etc.).
8 *Certainly* means 'definitely'. *Surely not* here is used to show that you can't believe that something is true – in this case that she's going to wear such a dress in public.
9 If something *fits* it is the right size. If something *suits* you it looks good on you.
10 Your *shadow* is the dark shape that appears behind you (or trees, buildings, etc.) when the sun is shining. *Shade* is the opposite of direct sunlight.
11 *Beside* means 'next to'. *Besides* means 'apart from'.
12 *To discover* something is to find something that already exists but is not known before (e.g. a planet, river). *To invent* something is to make up or produce something for the first time (e.g. a light bulb).

(continued on page 128)

Key

A 1a lend 1b borrow 2a raise 2b rise 3a steal 3b rob 4a lie 4b lay 5a winked 5b blinked 6a continual 6b continuous 7a room 7b space 8a surely 8b certainly 9a suit 9b fit 10a shadow 10b shade 11a beside 11b besides 12a invented 12b discovered 13a remember 13b Remind 14a alone 14b lonely 15a economical 15b economic

(continued on page 128)

36 Pairs of words that are often confused

A Here are fifteen pairs of words. Fill in the missing word in each sentence. (Make any verb tense changes that may be necessary.)

1 lend–borrow
   a I haven't got any money. Could you _____ me £10, please?
   b I often _____ books from the library.

2 rise–raise
   a Anyone who needs a lift home, please _____ your hand.
   b Do you think house prices will _____ soon?

3 rob–steal
   a Pickpockets usually find it easy to _____ from tourists – especially in large crowds.
   b Two masked men tried to _____ a bank this morning.

4 lie–lay
   a Does Swansea _____ to the east or the west of Cardiff?
   b She asked her daughter to _____ the table.

5 wink–blink
   a He _____ and smiled at the attractive woman sitting alone at the bar.
   b The child _____ when a bird suddenly flew close to his face.

6 continuous–continual
   a She found it hard to work because of the _____ hammering from the workmen doing repairs to the building opposite.
   b The brain needs a _____ supply of blood.

7 space–room
   a Their new flat was very small and there just wasn't enough _____ for all their furniture.
   b Leave lots of _____ between these shrubs when you plant them.

8 certainly–surely
   a You're _____ not going to wear that dress, are you? Not in public anyway!
   b I'm _____ not inviting Carol and David to my party. Not after the way they behaved last time.

9 fit–suit
   a Red doesn't really _____ me. I look much better in blue or yellow.
   b These shoes don't _____ – they're much too big.

10 shadow–shade
   a The building cast a long, dark _____.
   b It's hot. Let's go and sit in the _____ for a while.

11 beside–besides
   a He sat down in the park _____ an old woman.
   b Who else was at the meeting _____ Ken and Dave?

12 discover–invent
   a Thomas Edison _____ the light bulb.
   b Do you know who _____ the planet Pluto?

13 remember–remind
   a Did you _____ that it was Mandy's birthday today?
   b _____ me to send Mandy a birthday card, will you?

14 alone–lonely
   a Mrs Brown is a widow and lives _____.
   b People who feel _____ often get a dog or a cat to keep them company.

15 economic–economical
   a Small cars are usually more _____ than large ones.
   b The _____ situation in the country has improved in the last few months.

Teacher's notes

13 *To remember* is to recall from your memory. *To remind* is to tell someone to remember something.
14 If you live *alone*, you live on your own. If you feel *lonely*, you long for other people's company.
15 *Economic* is an adjective which means 'to do with the economy'. If something is *economical* it saves you money in some way by using less energy, petrol, etc.

Finally, give each pair of students one of the word pairs and ask them to write their own gapped sentence using one of the words only. Get them to write this sentence on a separate piece of paper. Allow 2–3 minutes, then collect all the papers, shuffle them and read them out loud, pausing after each one for the students to try to guess the missing word. (The students who wrote the sentence are, naturally, not allowed to guess!)

Practice (15 minutes)

Activity B Students work in groups. Give everyone a copy of the handout. They now write their own gapped sentences for these words, using Activity A as a guide. (They can use dictionaries, if necessary). When they have finished, they exchange papers with another group and try to fill in the missing words correctly. They hand their papers back to be marked. Who got them all right? If there is time, listen to one or two sentences from various groups at the end.

Conclusion (5 minutes)

Activity C Students work in pairs. Encourage them to work out what the missing words are without looking at previous exercises. Check orally.

Homework

Students work out the differences between the following:
bring–take
stationary–stationery
dialect–accent
libel–slander
solicitor–barrister
postpone–cancel

Key

B *Possible answers:*
1 The customs officer checked our passports. / Dogs and horses are sometimes very difficult to control.
2 Was it fun at the party on Saturday? / That film was very funny. It really made me laugh.
3 Did he give a reason for not coming to the meeting? / What was the cause of his illness?
4 As a child I used to collect stamps. / We went into the woods to gather blackberries.
5 I've got a marvellous recipe for meatballs. / If you keep your receipt, you can bring the shoes back if they don't fit.
6 Can I bring a friend to your party on Saturday? / Do you think you could take these books back to the library for me?

C 1 raise 2 beside 3 borrowed 4 invent 5 lie
6 economic 7 suit 8 shade

36 Pairs of words that are often confused
(continued)

B Make up sentences with gaps to show the difference in meaning between the following pairs of words. Write your sentences on a separate piece of paper. (Use a dictionary if necessary.)

1 check–control
2 fun–funny
3 reason–cause
4 collect–gather
5 recipe–receipt
6 bring–take

C Fill in the missing words.

1 We asked the speaker to r_____ her voice, as we couldn't hear her at the back.
2 Who's that sitting b_____ Cathy?
3 Don't forget to give me back that CD you b_____.
4 I wish someone would i_____ a machine that could do your homework for you.
5 The robber took out a gun and told everyone in the bank to l_____ face down on the floor.
6 Norway's e_____ position has improved considerably since they discovered oil in the North Sea.
7 I think I'll dye my hair black this time. Green hair didn't really s_____ me.
8 Shall we sit in the sun or in the s_____?

From *Instant Lessons 2 Intermediate* edited by Peter Watcyn-Jones © PENGUIN Books 2000

Teacher's notes

37 Prefixes

Aim	To show how prefixes are used in forming the opposites of adjectives.
Preparation	Copy the handouts on pages 131 and 133 – one copy per student.

Introduction (5 minutes)

Introduce the subject by writing the following on the board:
legal   conscious   possible   correct
Ask the students if they can give you the opposites of the above (*illegal, unconscious, impossible, incorrect*). Explain that *il-, un-, im-* and *in-* are called prefixes. Ask the students if they know any other adjectives that start with these prefixes. Add them to the board.
Tell the students that in this lesson you will be looking at various prefixes used with adjectives to give the opposites of the words.

Presentation (20 minutes)

Activity A Let the students work in pairs. Give everyone a copy of the handout. Explain what is to be done (do the first example orally in class, if necessary) then let them complete the exercise. Check orally, pointing out that the prefix *non-* is used differently from the other prefixes – a hyphen is needed to connect it to the adjective, for example *non-existent*.
As a quick revision, the students can test each other. One student reads out an adjective while his/her partner gives the opposite, using the correct prefix. They can take it in turns to read out and answer.

(continued on page 132)

Key

A dis- honest, loyal, satisfied
   il- legal, literate, logical
   im- mature, patient, possible
   in- accurate, considerate, correct, dependent, experienced, sane, sincere
   ir- regular, relevant, responsible
   mis- understood
   non- existent, resident, violent
   un- avoidable, comfortable, conscious, employed, necessary, popular, ripe

(continued on page 132)

37 Prefixes

A Which prefix would you put in front of these adjectives? Arrange the words under the correct headings. (The number in brackets after each heading says how many words are needed.)

accurate   avoidable   comfortable   conscious   considerate   correct
dependent   employed   existent   experienced   honest   legal   literate   logical
loyal   mature   necessary   patient   popular   possible   regular   relevant
resident   responsible   ripe   sane   satisfied   sincere   understood   violent

dis- (3)

in- (7)

non- (3)

il- (3)

un- (7)

im- (3)

ir- (3)

mis- (1)

Teacher's notes

Practice (15 minutes)

Activity B This is an exercise to check that they have learnt the words in Activity A. It can be done individually or in pairs. Give each student/pair a copy of the handout. Go through the first one with the whole class, then let them complete the rest. Check orally.

Conclusion (10 minutes)

Activity C This is an open-ended activity. Tell them to fill in the gaps using their own words. When they have finished, they find a partner and compare answers.

Homework

Ask the students to write sentences about themselves, their family, etc. using five of the words learnt during the lesson (i.e. including the prefixes).

Key

B 1 illiterate   2 unavoidable   3 uncomfortable
4 incorrect   5 dishonest   6 unpopular   7 irregular
8 non-resident   9 unconscious   10 inconsiderate
11 unemployed   12 illegal   13 immature
14 unnecessary   15 impossible   16 irresponsible
17 misunderstood   18 non-violent   19 independent
20 inexperienced

37 Prefixes (continued)

B Fill in the missing adjectives in the following sentences. (They are all to be found in Activity A.) To help you, the start of the words are given for sentences 1–10.

1. If you are unable to read or write, you are *il_____*.
2. The accident couldn't be helped. It was *un_____*.
3. What an *un_____* chair! I'd hate to sit on this for too long!
4. Sorry, that answer is *in_____*. Please try again.
5. It was very *dis _____* of him to keep the money.
6. The present government is very *un_____* at the moment. In a recent poll, only 15% of the population think they are doing a good job.
7. My visits to church are very *ir_____* – just once or twice a year, maybe.
8. Since he was a *non- _____* he didn't have to pay income tax.
9. The boxer was knocked *un_____*.
10. It was very *in_____* of you not to phone me to say you would be late coming home for dinner.
11. My uncle lost his job just before Christmas, and has been _____ ever since.
12. It is _____ in Britain to buy alcohol at a pub if you are under eighteen.
13. Generally speaking, boys at the age of thirteen are more _____ than girls of the same age.
14. You don't need to meet me at the airport – it's quite _____.
15. They say it is _____ to sneeze and keep your eyes open at the same time.
16. It was very _____ of your sister to let the children play with matches.
17. That's not what I meant. I've been _____ again!
18. They didn't believe in fighting. They preferred to solve problems using _____ means.
19. Our country has been _____ since 1965. That's when the French left.
20. They told her she was too _____ for the job. They needed someone who had taught for at least two years.

C Fill in the gaps using your own words.

1. It was very *inconsiderate* of him to _____.
2. _____ is *unavoidable*.
3. People who are *unemployed* should _____.
4. In my country, it is *illegal* to _____.
5. I get very *impatient* when _____.
6. One of the most *unpopular* people in my country is _____. He/she is unpopular because _____.
7. It is *impossible* to _____.
8. I was once very *dissatisfied* with _____.
9. An example of *immature* behaviour is _____.
10. Of all the things ever invented, _____ must be the most *unnecessary* one.

Teacher's notes

38 Giving definitions

Aim	To practise giving exact definitions for various nouns, verbs and adjectives.
Preparation	Copy the handouts on pages 135 and 137 – one copy per pair. Copy and cut up the handout on page 139 – one copy per student.

Introduction *(5 minutes)*

Write the following on the board:
NOUNS: binoculars, orchard, estuary
VERBS: collide, trespass, volunteer
ADJECTIVES: superstitious, illegible, temporary
Tell the students that you are going to read out six definitions – two for nouns, two for verbs and two for adjectives. After you have read each one, tell them to write what they think the word is on a separate piece of paper. When you have read out all six definitions, check orally. Explain any new words.
1 The mouth of a large river – the wide part that goes into the sea.
2 Believing in luck, chance and magic happenings.
3 A place where fruit trees are grown.
4 To offer to do something without being asked.
5 Lasting, or intended to last, only for a short time – in other words, not permanent.
6 To go on someone's private land without permission.

Presentation *(20 minutes)*

Activity A Students work in pairs – Student 1 and Student 2. Give everyone a copy of the appropriate handout. Explain what is to be done and allow time for preparation. Student 1 starts. If there is time, they can change papers and do it again. (It is surprising how many words will be remembered the second time!)

(continued on page 136)

Key

Introduction
1 estuary   2 superstitious   3 orchard   4 volunteer
5 temporary   6 trespass

(continued on page 136)

38 Giving definitions

A Student 1

Read out the following definitions to Student 2. See if s/he can guess the right answer. If not, tell him/her what the word is. Give 1 point for each correct answer. You can read out the definitions in any order.

Which (noun/verb/adjective) means ...?

NOUNS

1. A copy of a document, painting, bank note, etc. that has been made to deceive people. (*forgery*)
2. A long journey by sea. (*voyage*)
3. The killing of someone legally as a punishment for a serious crime, e.g. murder. (*execution*)
4. A sudden fall of rocks or snow down the side of a mountain. (*avalanche*)
5. A list of things to be dealt with or discussed at a meeting. (*agenda*)

VERBS

1. To vanish; to be seen no more. (*disappear*)
2. To take no notice of someone or something deliberately. (*ignore*)
3. To become red in the face, especially when you are embarrassed. (*blush*)
4. To get money or favours from someone by threatening to tell secrets about him/her. (*blackmail*)
5. To stop something from happening or to stop someone from doing something. (*prevent*)

ADJECTIVES

1. So silly as to make people laugh. (*ridiculous*)
2. Feeling sad because you are away from your home. (*homesick*)
3. Happening every year or once a year. (*annual*)
4. Not real; existing only in a person's mind. (*imaginary*)
5. Rather wet; not quite dry. (*damp*)

Now it is Student 2's turn to read out 15 definitions. As you listen, try to work out which words are being defined. Choose your answers from the following. (Only 15 of the words will be used!)

NOUNS: blizzard, corpse, currency, rumour, sleet, slogan, stench
VERBS: compete, confess, estimate, fade, inherit, solve
ADJECTIVES: bilingual, furious, lame, punctual, remote, scarce, urgent

When you have finished, compare scores. Who won?

Teacher's notes

Activity A The page opposite is the handout for Student 2.

(continued on page 138)

38 Giving definitions (continued)

A Student 2

Student 1 is going to read out 15 definitions. As you listen, try to work out which words are being defined. Choose your answers from the following. (Only 15 of the words will be used!)

NOUNS: agenda, anniversary, avalanche, execution, drought, forgery, voyage
VERBS: admire, blush, disappear, blackmail, grip, ignore, prevent
ADJECTIVES: annual, damp, homesick, imaginary, invisible, ridiculous

Now it is your turn to read out definitions to Student 1. Read out the following and see if s/he can guess the right answer. If not, tell him/her what the word is. Give 1 point for each correct answer. You can read out the definitions in any order.

Which (noun/verb/adjective) means ...?

NOUNS	VERBS	ADJECTIVES
1 The type of money that a particular country uses. Pounds and pence in Britain, dollars and cents in America, etc. (*currency*)	1 To make a guess about the amount, weight or value of something. (*estimate*)	1 Unable to walk properly because your leg or foot is injured or weak. (*lame*)
2 A short, catchy phrase used by an advertiser, politician, etc. (*slogan*)	2 To receive money, property, etc. from someone after s/he has died. (*inherit*)	2 Not available in sufficient numbers or not seen or found very often. (*scarce*)
3 A severe snowstorm. (*blizzard*)	3 To admit that you have done something wrong. (*confess*)	3 Able to speak two languages equally well. (*bilingual*)
4 A terrible smell. (*stench*)	4 To lose colour and brightness or to gradually disappear. (*fade*)	4 Arriving or happening at exactly the time that has been arranged. (*punctual*)
5 Information that is passed from one person to another and which may or may not be true. (*rumour*)	5 To find the answer to a problem or puzzle. (*solve*)	5 Extremely angry. (*furious*)

When you have finished, compare scores. Who won?

Teacher's notes

Practice (15 minutes)

Activity B This is a quick revision exercise. Students can work individually or in pairs. Give each student/pair a copy of the handout. Without looking back at Activity A, they try to work out what the missing words are. Do the first one orally in class, then let them complete the rest. Check orally.

Conclusion (10 minutes)

Activity C A final quick revision exercise for pairs – Student 1 and Student 2. Give everyone a copy of the appropriate handout. Explain that they have to make their partner say the five words they have on their cards by explaining them, miming them, etc. Student 1 starts.

Homework

Students use a dictionary to find definitions for the following (plus an example sentence):
anniversary
corpse
drought
sleet
admire
compete
grip
invisible
remote
urgent

Key

B 1 stench   2 currency   3 slogan   4 Execution
   5 prevent   6 disappear   7 damp   8 imaginary
   9 ridiculous   10 agenda   11 blackmail   12 forgery
   13 fade   14 solving   15 lame   16 scarce
   17 avalanche   18 rumour   19 blush   20 confessed
   21 annual   22 punctual   23 blizzard   24 estimated
   25 inherit   26 furious   27 voyage   28 ignore
   29 bilingual   30 homesick

38 Giving definitions (continued)

B What are the missing words in each sentence? To help you, some of the letters in each word are given.

1. What a s _ _ _ _ h! Open all the windows!
2. 'What is the c _ r _ _ _ _ y of Spain?' 'Pesetas, I think.'
3. 'Come alive with Pepsi!' is a famous advertising s _ _ g _ _.
4. 'How do they punish murderers in your country?' '_ x _ c _ t _ _ _.'
5. Not enough is being done to p _ _ v _ _ t road accidents.
6. Hundreds of young people d _ s _ _ p _ _ r without trace every year.
7. The cellar was very d _ _ _.
8. The equator is an _ m _ g _ _ _ _ y line running around the centre of the Earth.
9. You can't wear that dress! You look absolutely r _ d _ _ _ l _ _ s!
10. Right, let's get onto the next item on the _ g _ n _ a, shall we?
11. She tried to b _ _ _ k _ _ _ l the politician because of the secrets she knew about him.
12. On closer examination, the Hitler diaries were declared to be a f _ _ g _ _ y.
13. The curtain had been exposed to bright sunshine and was beginning to f _ _ _.
14. My uncle is very good at s _ _ v _ _ g crosswords.
15. The horse was l _ _ _ so he couldn't take part in the race.
16. For some reason, mushrooms are very s _ _ r _ e this year. That's why they cost so much in the shops.
17. Three skiers were killed in the recent _ v _ l _ _ ch _ in Austria.
18. There is a r _ m _ _ r going round that Microsoft is planning to take over IBM.
19. I always b _ _ _ h when I'm embarrassed.
20. The child finally broke down and c _ _ f _ _ s _ d that she had broken the vase.
21. Wimbledon is an _ n _ _ _ l tennis event, held in June and July.
22. This is an important meeting, so try to be p _ _ ct _ _ l for once!
23. It was impossible to drive during the b _ _ z _ _ _ d.
24. We e _ t _ m _ _ _ d that there were at least 25,000 people at the demonstration.
25. When his father dies he'll _ n _ _ r _ t at least £2 million.
26. My father was f _ r _ _ _ s when he found out that I had been arrested for shoplifting.
27. Before aeroplanes, the v _ y _ _ e to Australia could take up to six weeks.
28. When people are rude to me, I usually ig _ _ r _ them.
29. My brother is b _ l _ _ g _ _ l. He can speak English and French fluently.
30. My sister always gets h _ _ _ s _ _ k when she goes abroad.

C Student 1

1. stench
2. execution
3. blush
4. punctual
5. furious

C Student 2

1. blackmail
2. blizzard
3. inherit
4. rumour
5. lame

From *Instant Lessons 2 Intermediate* edited by Peter Watcyn-Jones © Penguin Books 2000

Teacher's notes

39 Phrasal verbs with *up*

Aim	To teach and practise some common phrasal verbs with *up* (*give up, turn up*, etc.).
Preparation	Copy the handout on page 141 – one copy per student or pair.

Introduction *(5 minutes)*

Introduce the subject by writing the following on the board:
I usually ____ up at 7.30 every morning.
Don't leave your things on the floor. ____ them up!
The taxi ____ up outside the station.
Ask the students if they can suggest verbs that will fill the gaps (answer: *get, pick, pulled/drew*). Explain that *get up, pick up* and *pull up* are all phrasal verbs. Ask them if they know any other phrasal verbs with *up*. Write them on the board. Tell the students that in today's lesson you will be looking at other phrasal verbs with *up*.

Presentation *(15 minutes)*

Activity A Let the students work in pairs. Give each pair a copy of the handout. Tell them to match the verbs with their definitions. Check orally, then let them test each other by taking it in turns to read out a definition and see if their partner can give the correct phrasal verb.

Practice *(20 minutes)*

Activity B Divide the class into groups of three or four. In groups, they discuss each of the questions, taking it in turns to give their opinions. Stop them after about 12 minutes.

Activity C Still working in groups, they decide if the phrasal verbs are used correctly. Check orally.

Conclusion *(10 minutes)*

A quick revision exercise. Read out the following sentences. After each one, pause and ask students to suggest a phrasal verb that can be used.
 1 We're going to decorate the kitchen this weekend.
 2 He was attacked and hit badly as he left the nightclub.
 3 If you don't know what the word means, find out from the dictionary.
 4 Nowadays more and more children are being raised by a single parent.
 5 Could I sleep at your place tonight?
 6 The terrorists destroyed the bridge using dynamite.
 7 Pam and Cathy didn't arrive until well after midnight.
 8 One day I'm going to stop smoking!
 9 My school closes for the summer on June 12th.
 10 Sorry I'm late. I was delayed by a traffic jam on the motorway.

Homework

Students use their dictionaries to find out what the following phrasal verbs mean. Ask them to write sentences of their own using each one.
come up
fix up
hang up
hurry up
own up
take up

Key

A 1 e   2 k   3 o   4 h   5 l   6 d   7 p   8 a   9 m   10 i
   11 b   12 f   13 n   14 c   15 j   16 g
C 1 No   2 Yes   3 No   4 No   5 Yes   6 Yes   7 Yes   8 No

Conclusion
1 do up   2 beaten up   3 look it up in   4 brought up
5 Could you put me up   6 blew up   7 turn up
8 give up   9 breaks up   10 held up

39 Phrasal verbs with *up*

A Match the phrasal verbs on the left with the correct definition on the right. Write your answers in the boxes below.

1	beat up	a	decorate (*a room*)
2	blow up	b	behave like an adult (*rather than behaving childishly*)
3	break up	c	become friends again (*after a quarrel*)
4	bring up	d	become happy (*after being sad*)
5	brush up	e	attack and hit someone badly
6	cheer up	f	delay
7	clear up	g	arrive
8	do up	h	raise (*children*)
9	dress up	i	stop doing something (*e.g. smoking*)
10	give up	j	give someone a bed for the night
11	grow up	k	destroy with explosives (*e.g. a bridge*)
12	hold up	l	practise and improve (*e.g. a foreign language*)
13	look up	m	put on your best clothes; wear a fancy-dress costume
14	make up	n	find information in a reference book (*e.g. the meaning of a word in a dictionary*)
15	put up	o	stop for the summer (*school*)
16	turn up	p	stop raining; turn sunny (*weather*)

1	2	3	4	5	6	7	8	9	10	11	12	13	14	15	16

B Discuss the following.

1. What was the last word in English you *looked up* in the dictionary? Which of the following words would you need to look up?
   valuable   to scold   consequently   niece   humid   illiterate
2. Have you ever *turned up* late for an important meeting or appointment? If so, what happened? Think of a good excuse for turning up late for the following:
   a job interview   an important exam   your own wedding
3. Write five dos and don'ts for parents *bringing up* children nowadays.
4. Have you ever tried to *give up* something, e.g. smoking? What happened? Were you successful? What advice would you give to someone who was trying to give up smoking or eating sweets and chocolates?
5. Name some occasions when it is necessary to *dress up*. What about fancy-dress parties? If you were invited to one, what (a) would you like to *dress up* as (b) wouldn't you dare *dress up* as?
6. If you were asked to *do up* this room, what would you do? (Think about the colour of the walls, curtains, carpets, furniture, etc.)

C Are the phrasal verbs used correctly in the following sentences? Answer *Yes* or *No*.

1. Most people would enjoy being *beaten up*. _____
2. Every morning my sister spends an hour in the bathroom and *holds me up*. _____
3. The team always plays better when there are lots of fans to *cheer them up*. _____
4. After you quarrel, it is nice to *blow up*. _____
5. Do you think children *grow up* too quickly these days? _____
6. Schools in Britain usually *break up* in July. _____
7. Don't stay at a hotel. We can *put you up*. _____
8. My room's very untidy. I'd better *brush it up*. _____

Teacher's notes

40 Types of people

Aim	To look at different types of people, e.g. *lodger, successor, hostage*, etc.
Preparation	Copy, cut up and shuffle the cards on pages 143 and 144 – one copy per pair.

Introduction *(5 minutes)*

Write the following on the board:
Mr Brown is my successor.
I am Mr Brown's predecessor.
Ask the students if they can work out what the words *successor* and *predecessor* mean (*successor* = the person who takes over your job from you when you leave; *predecessor* = the person who had your present job before you).
If necessary, help the students by giving extra clues. For example:
Mr Brown is my successor. He took over from me two weeks ago. I was very sorry to leave the job, etc.
Say that in today's lesson you will be looking at words for different types of people.

Presentation *(20 minutes)*

Let the students work in pairs. Give each pair a set of cards. Tell them to place the people on the left and the correct definitions on the right. Check orally by asking pairs in turns to suggest a 'correct' matching. If wrong, don't tell them the correct answer but go on to another pair. Continue until all the pairs are matched up correctly – even if it means the students have guessed in some cases.

Practice *(15 minutes)*

Students continue to work in pairs. The definition cards are shuffled and laid face down on the table in a pile. The 'types of people' cards are spread out on the table, face up. One student starts. He/she takes the top definition, reads it out and asks his/her partner for the type of person that matches the description. The student points to a card and, if it's the correct answer, keeps both the type of person card and the definition card. If not, the definition card is placed at the bottom of the pile to be used later. (If the students are not sure if an answer is correct or not, they call for the teacher.)

Continue like this, taking it in turns to read out a definition and guessing what the word is. Stop after 15 minutes. The student with the most cards is the winner.

Conclusion *(10 minutes)*

The teacher reads out the following sentences and the students write down the missing words on a separate piece of paper.
1 There were at least two hundred __(bleep!)___ waiting at the factory gates, trying to stop people working during the strike.
2 I don't know her all that well. She's just an __(bleep!)___.
3 My uncle's a real __(bleep!)___. He never spends any money if he can help it.
4 Tom rents a room at our house. He's been our __(bleep!)___ now for nearly five years.
5 This street is only for __(bleep!)___. Cars are not allowed.
6 Ralph McTell wrote his famous song 'The Streets of London' when he was a __(bleep!)___.
7 A small baby was the only __(bleep!)___ of the plane crash. Everyone else was killed.
8 I'd much rather play football than watch it. I don't enjoy being a __(bleep!)___.
9 The police told his __(bleep!)___ about the accident.
10 Reports are coming in that an unknown __(bleep!)___ has just killed the Prime Minister.

Homework

Students look up in their dictionaries what the following are and write a key sentence for each:
blackmailer
celebrity
genius
hooligan
opponent
rival

Key

Presentation
The cards are in the 'correct' order as laid out here. So remember to shuffle them before giving them out.

Conclusion
1 pickets 2 acquaintance 3 miser 4 lodger 5 pedestrians
6 busker 7 survivor 8 spectator 9 next-of-kin 10 assassin

40 Types of people

acquaintance	Someone you know, but not well enough to be called a friend.
assassin	Someone who murders for money or for political reasons.
bully	Someone who picks on or hits smaller or weaker people.
busker	A musician who plays in the street, at underground stations, etc.
deserter	A soldier who runs away from the army.
fugitive	Someone who is running away or hiding, often from the law.
hostage	Someone who has been captured by a person or organization and may be killed unless certain demands are met.
interpreter	Someone who translates the words a person is speaking into another language at the same time as the person is speaking.
lodger	Someone who rents a room with a family.
midwife	Someone who helps women when they are giving birth to babies.

40 Types of people (continued)

miser	Someone who loves money and really hates spending it.
next-of-kin	Your closest relative. If you are married, it would be your husband or wife.
participant	Someone who takes part in a contest, course, etc.
pedestrian	Someone who goes about on foot.
picket	Someone on strike who stands at the entrance to a factory trying to persuade other workers not to carry on working.
refugee	Someone who has been driven from their country for political reasons.
spectator	Someone who watches, for example, a football match, tennis match, etc.
stowaway	Someone who hides on board a ship or plane in order to travel without paying the fare.
survivor	Someone who is still alive after being involved in a plane crash, car accident, etc.
traitor	Someone who betrays his/her country.